Julie,

woo woo!
you are the best!
I've watched you learn
and grow into Being amazing
at what you do.

Always
Ticket to the limit

Randy C

TICKET

TO THE

LIMIT

TICKET
TO THE
LIMIT

HOW PASSION *and* PERFORMANCE CAN
TRANSFORM YOUR LIFE *and* YOUR BUSINESS
into an AMAZING ADVENTURE

RANDY COHEN
Chief Energizing Officer *of* TicketCity

EMERALD
BOOK CO.

Published by Emerald Book Company
Austin, TX
www.emeraldbookcompany.com

Distributed by Emerald Book Company

For ordering information or special discounts for bulk purchases, please contact Emerald Book Company at PO Box 91869, Austin, TX 78709, 512.891.6100.

Design and composition by Greenleaf Book Group LLC
Cover design by Greenleaf Book Group LLC

Publisher's Cataloging-In-Publication Data
(Prepared by The Donohue Group, Inc.)

Cohen, Randy (Randall Scott), 1965-
  Ticket to the limit : how passion and performance can transform your life and your business into an amazing adventure / Randy Cohen.-- 1st ed.

    p. ; cm.

ISBN: 978-1-934572-28-3

1. Work and family. 2. Quality of life. 3. Cohen, Randy (Randall Scott), 1965-
4. Chief executive officers--United States--Biography. 5. TicketCity (Firm).
I. Title.

HD4904.25 .C64
306.3/61   2009930348

Part of the Tree Neutral™ program, which offsets the number of trees consumed in the production and printing of this book by taking proactive steps, such as planting trees in direct proportion to the number of trees used: www.treeneutral.com

TreeNeutral

Printed in the United States of America on acid-free paper

09 10 11 12 13 14   10 9 8 7 6 5 4 3 2 1

First Edition

CONTENTS

INTRODUCTION
THE WOOWOO PHILOSOPHY AND RANDY'S RULES OF REASON

WOOWOO! STAND BACK NONBELIEVERS! What an incredible ride it's been so far! I'm one of those lucky people who have a ton of energy and can't wait to get out of bed each morning and dive into the day. What a great way to live! I think everyone—and I mean everyone—should have the opportunity to live an amazing life filled with fun and passion.

I realize that you may not be one of those fortunate folks who seize each day and love life, but why shouldn't you? Don't you deserve to have an amazing life? Don't you want to experience everything life has to offer and make a difference in the world? Wouldn't it be great to fully live the life you've imagined and always dreamed about? Of course it would!

This is what I call the "Woowoo" philosophy. The way I see it, you've got two choices: One is to complain, feel sorry for yourself, and be miserable. The other is to take life by the horns and make the absolute best of it—no matter who you are, where you are, or what you're doing. Abe Lincoln had it right more than a hundred years ago when he said, "A man's about as happy as he makes up his mind to be." That says it all.

Now, I may be accused of being an eternal optimist, but I think I'm having a lot more fun than all those "doom and gloom" folks. My Woowoo mentality has taken me pretty far, and I've had a great time along the way. I make a conscious decision to live with passion. I work at being positive and upbeat. I make the effort to find the good in things. I'm not saying that I'm always in a good mood or living in some happy-go-lucky fantasyland. And I certainly haven't cornered the market on optimism. You gotta work at it! However, if you practice being positive, you can actually develop the "habit" of being happy.

Why take my word for it? Well, I have figured a few things out after forty or so fabulous years on the planet. I've also had the unique opportunity to travel the world, meet some remarkable people, and experience some astonishing adventures. I've built a successful business on just $1,200 and some college basketball tickets. I've been to the greatest concerts and events in the world, hung out with celebrities, and met world-class athletes. I've been to the Olympic Games, Super Bowls, World Cup Championships, Kentucky Derbies, Masters Tournaments—you name it, I've done it!

A better experience lives here! That's the motto of my company, TicketCity, and it's a motto I use for my own life. Our mission is to provide our customers with the ultimate ticketing experience. We've grown from a few employees crammed around one computer to a staff of thirty-five in 10,000 feet of office space. Today we have 250,000 loyal and satisfied customers in seventy countries. We're bigger now, but we all share the same passion for excellence I had when I founded the company.

So, sure, I've squeezed a lot of living and learning out of life so far. And I want to continue to make a difference and share what I've learned. Maybe pass on a few tips and tidbits to help others live their ultimate lives. Share some secrets and lessons I've learned along the way . . .

For me, it all comes down to living your passion. Reaching your potential. Making a difference. Tackling life with energy and emotion. This may seem obvious, but then why do so few people live it? It's pretty easy for living big to get lost in the day-to-day chaos and confusion of life: Rush off to that meeting. Get the kids to football practice. Pick up some groceries.

Take that conference call. The trick is to find the joy: love what you do and stay passionate. Easier said than done!

Mastering the game of life is not for the timid. But if what I've found through trial and error, through building a business, or through some truly remarkable experiences can help others, then great!

RANDY'S RULES OF REASON

Passion is one of the keys to my success, but I've figured out a few other things during my forty-four years. I call these simple success secrets "Randy's Rules of Reason." I have organized this book around these ten rules. As you read each chapter, you will learn much more about how these rules worked for me and how they can also work for you. For now, here's a brief overview of my rules for living a great life.

1. BE PASSIONATE. LOVE WHAT YOU DO.

If you don't love what you do, you're not going to be very happy or successful. Maybe that sounds painfully obvious, but there are an awful lot of people out there who are miserable. Maybe they're in dead-end jobs and just slogging along through life. To escape that trap you've got to find something you love to do and then do it with passion. It's not easy, but the alternative is a life unfilled, void of pizzazz.

2. LIVE YOUR VALUES.

At some point in your life (now is good), you've got to look inside and reflect upon your core values. Then, you've got to walk the walk and live those values! You'll know whether you're on the right track, because your conscience will be your guide. Do you feel in sync and on your game? Then you're living your values!

3. PUT FAMILY FIRST.

With today's frenetic schedules, maintaining balance has become a real challenge—especially when it comes to family. You've got to keep things in perspective and make your family your top priority. You'll have many jobs or careers throughout your life, but you've got only one family. Always put them first.

4. TAKE CARE OF YOUR PEOPLE. FIND THE AMAZING.

You've got to look out for your people—this includes your family and friends. Take care of your people at the office, and they will repay you with loyalty and treat you like royalty. After all, most successful people didn't get to the top on their own. They got there by standing on the shoulders of others! Be good to your people and they will do good for you!

5. HAVE FUN. LEARN TO LAUGH!

Life can be a lot more fulfilling and enjoyable when you laugh often, have fun, and smile. Laughing is like exercise for the soul. It actually reduces stress and will help you live longer! Everybody wants to have fun, but believe it or not, fun doesn't always happen by itself. You've got to plan to have fun; you've got to be intentional about it. Be sure to put fun in your day and find plenty of reasons to laugh, even at yourself—especially at yourself!

6. HAVE A BIG HEART. MAKE A DIFFERENCE.

To live the life you truly desire, you've gotta have heart! Heart is that special something that separates Joe Montana or Joe Namath from the average Joe. It's that magical quality that keeps you going and puts you over the top. Having a big heart also means giving back and being kind. Think of the movie *Rudy*.

Closely related to having heart is making a difference. If love comes from the heart, then I suppose you could say that making a difference comes from the soul. In my less than humble opinion, you were not put on this Earth just to take care of yourself. You're here to enrich and enhance the lives of others. You're here to leave the world a little better than when you found it. You've got to try to make a difference.

7. NEVER STOP LEARNING.

One of the things I really look forward to every day is learning and growing. Learning is not a goal; it is a lifelong process. I believe we've all got an opportunity and an obligation to learn as much as we can while we're here. Knowledge breeds understanding, confidence, and compassion—all traits required for great success. As far as I'm concerned, when you stop learning, you stop living.

8. TAKE CHANCES. PUT YOURSELF OUT THERE.

One of the ways you can live "on purpose," is to simply put yourself out there. Take risks. Be bold. Try new things. Don't be afraid to make a fool of yourself from time to time—especially in pursuit of a worthy goal. And don't be afraid to fail, because no matter what, you will make mistakes and you will fall down. The trick is getting back up again. One of my favorite quotes simply states: "Success is falling down nine times and getting up ten!" You're not going to get ahead unless you put yourself out there.

9. BE A ROCK STAR! WORK HARD AND PLAY HARD.

I guess I'm from the old school: I agree with the simple and time-tested advice to work hard. Unless you were born into royalty or win the lottery, you're gonna have to work hard to succeed. The old cliché has never been more true. Work hard—and play hard! Why? Because how you do anything is how you do everything!

10. FOLLOW THROUGH. MASTER THE GAME.

Another key quality that separates the winners from the losers is follow-up and follow-through. It's simple: You've got to do what you say you're gonna do! Keep your commitments. Fulfill your obligations. Deliver on your promises. Better yet, over-deliver! Once you become a man or woman of your word, people will begin to know, like, and trust you. Then you're really on your way!

Now, let's get started learning to play (and win) by the rules. Get your own ticket to success! Woowoo, let's go!

Randy Cohen, 2009
Chief Energizing Officer
TicketCity

PASSION

RULE #1
BE PASSIONATE. LOVE WHAT YOU DO.

Desire is the starting point of all achievement, not a hope, not a wish,
but a keen pulsating desire which transcends everything.

—*Napoleon Hill*

AND THEY'RE OFF! It was my first Kentucky Derby: I was talking with Troy Aikman, meeting Pam Anderson and Kid Rock, and betting on the big race. Wow, what an adventure. Life sure was good.

Learn to fly. Swim with sharks. Go white-water rafting in Costa Rica. Attend a Brazil versus England soccer match. See the Rolling Stones in concert. Own a 1967 Shelby Mustang convertible. Play the Masters course at Augusta. Write a book—you're holding it in your hands!

You might be wondering what all the wild activities above have in common. They're all part of my 100 Things to Do in Life list. What? You don't have a Things to Do in Life list? Why not? How are you going to squeeze the most out of life if you don't make a list of the things you want to do before you die? Some people call it a "bucket list," but don't wait until your so-called "golden years" before you decide what you really want from life. Get going on your own list. C'mon, it's easy. Just use your imagination. Write down anything and everything you'd like to be, do, or have in life. Don't hold back. Think big.

I'm working my way through my list. Swim on the back of a giant sea turtle. Check. Jump out of a plane. Done. Attend the NCAA Final Four. Been there. Be on television. Done that. Visit every NFL stadium and major league baseball park. Working on it. Go on an African safari. Still gotta do that one.

Can't think of one hundred things? Start with twenty, or ten—just start your list! I'll admit that my 100 Things to Do in Life list includes some pretty outrageous goals, but there's a ton of stuff on my list that I've been lucky enough to experience: I'm a partner in a castle in India, so I can say I own a castle! I've been in a simulated dogfight in a fighter jet. I've been to world-class prizefights in Vegas; I've visited Cuba; I've been given a key to the city by the mayor; I've been scuba diving, sky diving, and bungee jumping. I've started companies, bought companies, and met celebrities and sports stars. How do I manage to do so many cool things? I just decide what I want to do, and I set out to do it. The more I do, the more I add to my list. There's still so much to do and experience!

Someday, I want to sail around the world with no cell phones, no Internet, and no distractions. I've always wanted to meet Sir Richard Branson and hang out with him on his private island. I still need to catch a foul ball or home run ball at a major league baseball game. Still gotta go on a submarine; still gotta shoot that elusive hole in one. I'm getting there, mostly because I was raised to believe in great possibilities. My life has been full of incredible opportunities, so the least I can do is try to pass on some ideas and advice to others who want the most from their lives.

I certainly don't claim to have all the answers, and I'm not perfect. But I love life, and I love seeing others reach their potential and find their passion. There's a lot I need to do better, and I'm working on that! I still want to start my own charity or foundation; I want to be the best father ever to my three children and give them a life of possibilities. But one day at a time, I'm doing the things I set out to do, and you can, too!

It doesn't matter where you're starting from or how old you are or how much money you make. I didn't inherit a fortune or win the lottery. I just knew what I wanted and I worked my butt off. Obviously, I had some help. No one succeeds on their own. (I'll talk more about that in the chapter on getting a coach.) I've taken some chances, and I've made plenty of mistakes. But let me share a few of the things that have worked for me over the years; I hope the advice in this book will help you and inspire you to accomplish the amazing things on your list.

START WITH PASSION

Woowoo! As you can probably tell, I'm an energetic guy, and I love life. I think passion is *the* critical element in living a great life. Dive into each day. Be passionate about everything you do. Dream big and pursue those dreams. Go big or go home! I could throw a hundred sayings at you, but the point is you've got one life and one chance to walk this earth, so you have to make it count.

I may have friends or colleagues who think I'm a little over the top, but isn't that more fun than trudging through life? Why shouldn't you live each precious day with passion? Do what you love and love what you do! Put yourself out there. Have some fun. Make a difference! Put some life into your life!

Maybe you're not the outgoing, gregarious type. That's fine. Don't confuse passion with personality. You don't have to be extroverted, fun-loving, or the life of the party to have passion. Look at Mother Teresa or Mahatma Gandhi. Did they live with passion and purpose? For every animated, passionate Donald Trump or Oprah Winfrey, there are hundreds of quiet, unknown, passionate people living lives of meaning and purpose.

That's the great thing about passion. You get to choose how you express it! You get to decide what living passionately means to you and then live each day according to your own standards. The important thing is to be present and to be aware. Think about what lights your fire, and don't lose sight of your dreams in the day-to-day routine of living.

Is passion something you're born with? That I don't know, but I do know it can be learned. You can learn to live with passion, and you can develop the habit of putting passion and enthusiasm into your life. You may need to step outside your comfort zone and push yourself, but the effort is worth it! It's as simple as being grateful for the things in your life. Gratitude is one surefire path to passion. Be thankful for every day and watch how quickly your outlook improves.

PASSION, THEN "CASH IN"

Don't expect to "cash in" before you've got the passion! That lust for life, that zest for zeal, is the real secret to fulfillment. *Do what you love*, as the old saying goes, *and the money will follow.*

What does passion represent to you? How do you capture that magical feeling? When I think of passion, I usually think of college sports. Students, alumni, and fans are very emotional about their college teams. There's so much energy and enthusiasm wrapped up in these events, and the fervor of the fans shines through. There are fierce loyalties and bitter rivalries. There's drama, suspense, excitement, and anticipation rolled up in every game. There are intense highs and lows, hopes and dreams—even miracles! As Jim McKay used to say in the introduction of *ABC's Wide World of Sports*, it's the "thrill of victory and the agony of defeat!"

I think back to the BCS college football championship game a few years ago in California. It was undefeated Texas against undefeated USC playing at the Rose Bowl for the national championship. Nothing beats the energy that college sports has to offer: the fans, the students, the atmosphere, and the location all provided for an amazing experience. TicketCity was fortunate to have a large number of tickets for that game, and what a game it was! We were able to make so many dreams come true, and it turned out to be one of the greatest games in college football history, with quarterback Vince Young leading the Texas Longhorns to the victory. The energy in Pasadena that day was spectacular, and the celebration was flowing freely. The excitement and electricity in the air was so thick you could cut it with a knife. All of this adds up to passion, passion, passion.

DRINKING THE KOOL-AID

How do you keep passion in what you do?

First, you've got to understand exactly what it is you do. At TicketCity, we do the following:

We sell tickets for all events, including sold-out events. Our tickets put our clients in premium seats—the best seats available—at the most exciting events in the world. Though we have tickets for all events, we specialize in college sports and championship events, such as the Masters, the Kentucky Derby, and the US Open.

We are a ticket broker that sells tickets at market value, not face value. That means our tickets often cost more; however, we have plenty of tickets listed at or below face value. Market price is determined by demand for a particular event; hot events can be pricey, while less popular events are more affordable.

We can supply our clients with everything to make their experience more memorable: the best seats in the house, exclusive hospitality passes, parking passes, VIP club passes, or travel arrangements.

We do our best to develop passion in our employees, and we're fortunate because we tend to hire people with that innate spark. We look for people with energy, drive, and enthusiasm, but we continue to coach them once they're on board. We put a lot of emphasis on training, and we give our employees the tools and resources they need to enhance their passion for what they do.

We give our employees the knowledge they need, and knowledge is power. They've been trained and coached and supported, and that breeds more confidence. With that confidence they become passionate. Suddenly, the staff is having fun, they're making money, they're doing a great job—so they bring their passion and enthusiasm to the office every day. Best of all, it's contagious, so it spreads to the entire team!

When your employees are engaged—when they drink the Kool-Aid, to use a popular analogy—you get more focus, enthusiasm, and drive from them. Once you build trust with your staff, that trust can be passed on to your customers. Inspired employees inspire customers!

We keep our employees motivated and fired up by keeping the work environment fun and by listening to them and acknowledging them. You've got to find the fun in everything you do—even at work. Figure out your "why." Why do you get up every morning? Why do you do what you do? What's your bigger purpose? Passion is within; you just have to tap into it.

If you love what you do, do it well, and keep doing it, then you're on the right track. When I jump out of bed every morning, I know I'm going to make a difference! I'm going to jazz up someone's world and make a dream come true! Maybe they've always dreamed of going to the Olympics or taking their child to her first major league baseball game. My company helps make those experiences possible.

My "why" is to make a difference in the lives of others; to connect people; to learn something new every day; to have fun; to make people smile; to be a great dad. Those core values help me live my life with passion and purpose. Find your "why" and you'll discover your passion.

GETTING FIRED UP!

How do you get fired up? Do you dive into each day? Do you live full out? For me, there's no other way to live. I never do anything halfway. I find a way to do the things I love to do, so it's easy to get excited and stay motivated. I surround myself with good people, and I maintain a positive outlook. Some of the best career advice I've ever heard is to determine what you truly enjoy doing and then find a way to get paid for it. If you're good at it, you'll get paid a lot to do it!

When you're fired up, you're full of energy and enthusiasm. Time flies by and work feels like play. Your job is almost effortless and you feel like you're in the zone. You've hit your stride. You're "on your game" and simply cruising along, enjoying the ride of life and making it look easy.

What if you can't find your "mojo"? How do you get back on track? Well, music always helps. Crank your favorite song. Spin it and spark it, jump up and down, dance, do a backflip. You may get a few weird looks if you're in public, but it will definitely put a smile on your face and on the faces of others, too! Keep a gratitude journal, and refer to it when you're down. If you remind yourself of all the good in your life, chances are you'll lighten your mood. Watch your favorite TV show or movie. Try watching the movies *Rudy* or *Top Gun* for surefire inspiration. Go shopping or buy

EXPERIENCING THE KENTUCKY DERBY

Seattle Slew, Affirmed, War Emblem, Smarty Jones, Giacomo, and Big Brown—these are just a few of the amazing horses that have won the Kentucky Derby. Since the first race was held in Louisville in 1875, the Kentucky Derby has become one of the world's premier sporting events, drawing more than 100,000 fans a year, with a record 163,628 fans attending in 1974. Though the race only lasts two minutes (Secretariat ran the race in the record time of 1:59.4 in 1973), the parties and events surrounding the Derby on the first weekend in May entice beautiful women in extravagant outfits and fashionably dressed men to enjoy mint juleps as they hang out in the Turf Club and wager on the races throughout the day.

The Kentucky Derby is one of TicketCity's most successful and passionate events. Tickets are sold for as much as $4,000 each in Millionaire's Row at ticketcity.com. Looking for a tip as to who will win the derby? Ninety-seven of the 130 or so winning horses were born in the bluegrass state of Kentucky. And if you consider the jockeys in your wagers, don't discount experience. Fifty-four-year-old Willie Shoemaker became the oldest jockey to win the Derby when he rode Ferdinand to victory in 1986.

yourself a new toy. You deserve it! Go out and treat yourself to an ice cream. If that still doesn't work, do a good deed. Help somebody out. A good deed will always fire you up! These are just a few of the ways you can get and stay fired up and feeling good.

YOUR STOCK JUST WENT UP

In addition to ambition, going above and beyond in service has always been part of my DNA. As a company, TicketCity has to provide the "wow!" We've got to create amazing experiences for people. That's true whether we're providing tickets to a once-in-a-lifetime event or whether we're hosting our own company function.

Every year we produce a major "wow" event—the TicketCity Invitational, a golf tournament popular with celebrities and other VIPs. Judging by the tournament's continued growth and the feedback we get, we're doing a good job of wowing people. Here's a copy of a thank-you note I received right after the 2008 event:

> May 13, 2008
>
> Your stock went up big time last Friday after you pulled off an amazing golf tournament. I had a blast, met some great guys, and was treated like royalty. Thank you for including me in such a wonderful event.
>
> Best regards,
> Randy H.

I'm a firm believer in creating the wow. If we create the wow for our customers, those customers are going to keep buying from us. You see, I believe we're not just selling tickets; we're building relationships!

LOVE WHAT YOU DO

It may seem obvious that one of the keys to success and happiness is to do what you love and love what you do. However, many of us spend a lifetime searching for a way to do those things we love to do. Some of us aren't even sure what it is that really makes us tick. If you can find a way to do what you love and love what you do, your life will be one of happiness, fun, and fulfillment.

How do you discover what you love to do? Maybe you already know and you're working on ways to do it more often. Perhaps you haven't quite discovered your passion and your purpose just yet, so maybe it's time for some soul searching.

Ask yourself a few important questions: What are you good at? What do you enjoy so much that it's almost effortless? What do you do better than anyone else? When does work seem more like play, with time flying when you're doing it? When do you feel most alive? Jeff and Rich Sloan, the "startupologists" at StartupNation.com, advise entrepreneurs to identify what they love and build a business around it.

Here's another quick exercise: If you could wave a magic wand to design your life exactly the way you wanted it, what would it look like? Where would you live? What would you be doing? Who would you be hanging out with? How would you spend your time? What would you own? What kinds of activities would you be involved in?

Maybe you love playing tennis. Think about how often you play. Can you find a way to play every day or, better yet, earn a living from it? If you love tennis, can you become a tennis instructor? Can you integrate your passion for tennis into other areas of your life?

Let's face it: if you're a golf fanatic and you live in Buffalo, New York, or Minneapolis, Minnesota, you'll probably get to play golf only four or five months a year. And if you're working seventy hours a week, you're not going to have much time to pursue your passion for golf. Do some serious self-assessment and figure out how to do more of what you want to do. Visualize your ideal future and then begin to take some steps to get there.

Conceive, believe, achieve! If you believe, like I do, that you create your own destiny and design your own life, then it's time to focus on what you want and start working toward living your "best-case scenario." What are you waiting for? *Abracadabra!* Make it happen!

Here's one more brief exercise to help you become the author of your own life story: Write your obituary or your eulogy. Sure, it's a bit maudlin, but give it a try. What will others say about you when you're gone? How will you be remembered? What did you accomplish? Has your life been ordinary or extraordinary? Did you lead a quiet, uneventful life, or was your life filled with adventure and excitement? Maybe you prefer a quiet life—that's fine—as long as that's what makes you happy.

Loving what you do doesn't necessarily mean jumping out of planes or finding a cure for cancer. It's what lights *your* fire. For you, it could be serving in the military or being a teacher or building houses or being an accountant. *You* get to decide what fires you up. But if you're that accountant who has a passion for tennis and always wanted to be a tennis instructor, what's holding you back? Will your gravestone say: "Always wanted to be a tennis pro, but I never got around to it"? You've got the opportunity to write your own story—and your own history—so make the most of it!

DREAMS AND GOALS

It's a whole lot easier to get fired up and live passionately when you've got dreams and goals. When setting goals, follow your heart. I love this Henry David Thoreau quote: "Go confidently in the direction of your dreams. Live the life you have imagined." You'll know if you've set the right goal because it will be something you can get really excited and energized about.

Goal setting should be a dynamic, ongoing process. A goal is not one destination. Goals are part of your larger journey on your way to achieving your dreams. So set goals and track your progress. Break your big, audacious goals down into more manageable milestones. Make that list of one hundred things you want to do, be, or accomplish before you die, and then begin checking things off the list.

GAME FILM

One of the best ways to reach your goals is through visualization—or what I like to refer to as "game film." All the great athletes do it, and you can do it, too! For example, Tiger Woods plays out his game in his mind with mental images of success before he ever gets to the course. In fact, studies have proven that your subconscious mind can't really distinguish the imagined event from the actual event! (Heck, Forrest Gump even became an Olympic ping-pong champion by "game filming" when he slept! Sure, it's a movie, but you get the idea.) Use your own positive mental visualization, or game filming, every day to self-improve. In your mind, just roll the tape and picture how you want your day to go. See yourself succeeding and hitting your goals. Play the game film over and over, until it's embedded in your subconscious. Try it, and see how it works!

You can game film both before and after an event. Football teams spend hours reviewing game film from the previous week's game so they can see what they did right and what they did wrong. This detailed analysis of the tape helps the players evaluate their progress and set new benchmarks for the next game. Study the film and see what needs work. Some coaches would even argue that the game is won or lost before the teams ever take the field! How's that for the power of visualization?

Speaking of football, don't you love those locker room celebrations after a team wins the Super Bowl or the World Series? You can really feel the excitement, the elation, and the pure joy that the players are experiencing. I think back to the 2004 World Series, when the Boston Red Sox finally won a championship after an eighty-six-year drought! The Sox had to overcome seemingly insurmountable challenges, not the least of which was coming back from a three-game deficit in the playoffs against their bitter rivals, the Yankees.

The Red Sox beat the odds and "reversed the curse of the Bambino" to come back and win it all. The difficulty of that victory made the celebration even sweeter. I'm sure you remember the images of champagne spewing all over the locker room and Big Papi wearing swimming goggles to keep the champagne out of his eyes. Now that was a party!

Wouldn't it be amazing if we celebrated everyday life just as passionately? Now, I'm not suggesting that we pour champagne over our heads on a regular basis, but we do need to learn to celebrate more often.

AMAZING PROFILES: ROY SPENCE

I'm blessed to have some truly amazing friends and colleagues, and throughout this book, I'd like to introduce you to a few of them. These remarkable men and women live and breathe passion, and they create a "wow" in everything they do. One such rock star is Roy Spence, the Idea Man.

Roy is a cofounder and the current CEO of GSD&M, a little ad agency based in Austin, Texas, that handles the advertising for some companies you may have heard of: Southwest Airlines, AT&T, Wal-Mart, MasterCard, BMW, and the United States Air Force, just to name a few.

Roy and his partners started their agency right out of college with what they recall as "six kids with no money" but plenty of youthful bravado. Today, GSD&M employs 650 people and has revenues of $1.5 billion. (Yes, billion with a *b*). Roy inspires his family of employees to the point that they call him "Reverend Roy," and he's affectionately known as the "Idea Man" by his colleagues. His office is called "Idea City"!

Roy provides the passion, drive, and raw energy for his company. He inspires and leads his troops with motivating "Royisms," and he insists on hiring "doers and dreamers and no in-betweeners." Here's what he has to say about hiring the right people, and I couldn't agree more:

> If we hire the right people and put them in a place where they can win— if we let them do the things they are passionate about, the things that make economic sense—if we surround ourselves with people who share our values, standards, and ideals—then we will generate unlimited ideas and opportunities. And we will become a great company. If we don't embark upon greatness, we will not survive by just being good.

Roy is definitely a maverick who blazes his own trail and who takes pride in turning small opportunities into big successes. As you might imagine, he's also a huge proponent of teamwork and partnerships. As far back as high school, Roy was a leader and fierce competitor. He became his football team's quarterback not because of his size, but as a result of sheer willpower. That team went on to win the state championship.

He attended the University of Texas, and years later he helped the city of Austin get behind the UT's Longhorns and quarterback Vince Young during the team's 2005–2006 Rose Bowl championship season by teaching everyone to live the dream. Roy Spence personifies the belief of doing what you love and loving what you do.

Before we move on, I'd like to share a few of my favorite "Royisms":

"What a company stands for is as important as what it sells."

"If you want froufrou advertising, hire the other guy. We say, 'get rid of the fancy-pants suits with Ivy League degrees.' What we do is kick some butt for clients."

"In the end, we're on a relentless mission to find visionary ideas that get our clients where they want to be faster than they thought possible. That sounds audacious. But if you don't have audacious goals, your people will be status quo instead of status go."

"We ride at dawn!"

"I believe that ideas are going to be the currency of the twenty-first century; corporate cultures are going to be the competitive advantage. We spend an enormous amount of time on our creative culture."

"I like to plant seeds. I've made a lot of mistakes, but my feeling is that in this business you're growing only if you're creating."

"Losing sucks. I'm not one of those who thinks that just getting there is victory."

RULE #2
LIVE YOUR VALUES.

The spirit, the will to win, and the will to excel are the things that endure. These qualities are so much more important than the events that occur.

—*Vince Lombardi*

IT WAS THE 2006 WORLD CUP in Germany. The World Cup had not been played in Europe since 1998, and the energy in the city was electric. The TicketCity office was stationed in downtown Frankfurt, and we were ready to rock and roll: we had ample inventory, a great location, and plenty of customers still needing tickets.

From June 9 to July 9, daily World Cup soccer matches were held throughout the country, and my team had to be poised to jump on a train at a moment's notice to go to wherever a particular game was being played. My team members traveled to Leipzig, Hamburg, Cologne, Dortmund, Hanover, Berlin, Munich, Gelsenkirchen, Nuremberg, and Stuttgart to deliver or pick up tickets. A lot of money was at stake, and the TicketCity team was like a finely tuned engine. Everyone knew their responsibilities, and they knew we stood to make a lot of money if we could make this World Cup a successful event. We worked fourteen-hour days and then had great meals together in the evenings where we talked about the day's experiences and prepared for the next day. We made adjustments and sent people in different directions in order to give the best customer service possible.

During the matches, employees were able to take breaks to watch some of their favorite teams, including England, Brazil, Italy, Mexico, Germany, Argentina, and the United States. We also gave everyone a few days off so they could travel around Europe and see the sights. I even took off a few days and traveled with a few of the fellas to Prague for a little R and R. The World Cup event turned out to be the most successful event in the history of TicketCity. We made nearly $2 million, and everyone received amazing bonuses and had the time of their lives.

CORE VALUES

Live your values. This sounds simple enough, but it's easy to get sidetracked. How do you know whether you're living your values? First, you've got to determine what your core values are. Then you've got to check in with yourself—do an honest self-assessment—and make sure you're walking the walk. Review, reflect, and recommit weekly—or monthly—whatever works for you to stay on track. Just check in at regular intervals to make sure that you're truly living by your values.

Your core values should be what *you* decide, not what you think others expect them to be. Your core values don't necessarily need to be lofty or noble, though it's great if they are. Your values just need to be authentic to you. You can't live someone else's values. Be true to yourself, and that will feed your enthusiasm and passion.

For instance, one of my core values is having fun, but the kind of fun I like to have often requires money. Money means freedom and flexibility to me. Money brings a certain amount of empowerment and choice. So don't be afraid to admit to yourself that money matters. Making money enables me to have fun, travel, and make a difference in the lives of others. Having money makes some of my other core values possible.

My other core values include continuing to learn and grow, both personally and professionally; to be a good parent and spend time with my children; to be healthy; to laugh as much as possible; and to make a difference in the world.

My core values are posted on my computer. My electronic calendar reminds me once a week to review my core values to stay true to myself. This way I make sure I reflect on my core values and walk the talk. This gives me an opportunity to review, reflect, and recommit. Then I can look back on the week, consider those things that are important to me, and ask myself, "Was I a good parent this week? Did I make a difference? Did I laugh and have fun? Was I healthy? How can I do better? What can I do to improve?" Regular self-assessment is important to make sure you're living your core values. Core values are so important to me that I take every opportunity to talk about them, even to the press.

INC. 5,000 LIST OF FASTEST-GROWING COMPANIES RECOGNIZES TICKETCITY

TicketCity ranks No. 2,772 on the 2007 Inc. 5,000 List, and No. 3,892 on the 2008 List

Austin, TX—*Inc.* ranked TicketCity at 2,772 on its first-ever Inc. 5,000 list of the fastest-growing private companies in the country. Growing at an annual rate of 45% each year over the last three years, TicketCity remains a leader in the secondary ticketing industry.

Randy Cohen, founder and current CEO, grew TicketCity from selling a few UT tickets in the early '90s to establishing a multimillion-dollar international ticketing business. "Our continued success results from maintaining our core values while carefully managing growth," comments Cohen. "We've seen much success . . . and we will continue to strive for better while maintaining our core values of excellent service and quality ticket inventory."

It's one thing to figure out your core values and write them down, but it's another to review them often enough to keep yourself on track. A lot of companies and corporations spend all kinds of time and money coming up with a mission statement that then gets filed away, not to be looked at for years. A mission statement is nothing more than your values spelled out. If you're going to go to the effort of making a personal mission statement or listing your core values, be sure to keep that statement or list front and center. Look at it every week, if not every single day. Review your list and "renew your vows." Remember, the more you truly live your values, the more passion and energy you're going to have in your life.

Some of your core values have been with you for almost your entire life. You may have picked them up from your parents or family or developed them along the way. You may have integrated them over time. At some point, your values become so ingrained that they define who you are.

For example, ever since I was a kid I've always liked coming up with schemes to make money. Each summer I visited my grandma in Scituate, Massachusetts, on the South Shore, not far from Cape Cod. As far back as I can remember, I'd go down to the beach at low tide and collect sea glass. Every day, when the tide went out, I'd search for the colorful pieces of sea glass because I knew I could sell them for money. I'd fill tall glass containers with sea glass and then sell it for change.

Later on, I'd set up a lemonade stand and sell lemonade by the side of the road. I was pretty industrious as a kid, and as I got older, I'd seek other ways to make money during the summer. There was always a parking crunch at the beach, so I'd approach the cars and get them to park on the lot at our cottage. I'd think, *Hey, we can get fifty cars parked back here in our field and charge $3 per car. That's $150 bucks!* But I did have to split my revenue with my grandma since she owned the joint.

Then, as a teen, I worked at the Rocking Horse Ranch in Upstate New York as a waiter and a busboy. I remember getting $20 tips for going above and beyond. So I learned at a young age that if you do good things for people—if you really take care of them—it pays off. You get rewarded for hard work and extra effort. So you could say my work ethic and ambition has been with me all my life!

CELEBRATE

Life isn't all about working. It should be all about celebrating. Not just dreaming, but doing! Not just watching, but participating. Not just going along for the ride, but grabbing the wheel and really going places! I'm sure you can see the distinction here. Life is to be savored and celebrated.

One of the ways to squeeze the most out of life is to banish your fears and take chances. Be guided by your faith and not your fear. Put yourself out there! Be a difference maker. Be fearless and courageous.

Putting yourself out there isn't always easy. It's sometimes embarrassing. You'll probably have butterflies in your stomach—but that's a good sign that you're pushing yourself. I'm the type of guy who will get up in front of six hundred people at a conference or event and ask a question. I'll also seize the opportunity to give a plug for my company! I'll jump up in front of an auditorium full of people and say, "Hi, I'm Randy Cohen with TicketCity, where you get the best of tickets for the best of times!"

Heck, I'm even willing to put myself out there and possibly make a fool of myself on national television! I once appeared on *The Montel Williams Show*. It was a segment called "Who Wants to Marry a Millionaire?" based on the reality show. I seized my moment in the spotlight and told the world, "Hello, I'm Randy Cohen from TicketCity, where you get the best of tickets for the best of times, America." We received so many hits to our website that it crashed our servers! But that's the type of stuff you've got to do to seize life and make the most of it.

I'm not one to shy away from opportunities—especially if it means smart publicity for my company. I'm proud of TicketCity's success and want to share our story with everyone. One of my favorite moments was at an awards ceremony when TicketCity was named one of the fastest-growing companies by the *Austin Business Journal*. (We won this award six years in a row!) The *Austin Business Journal* always brought in guest speakers for the awards ceremony, but I boldly suggested that they let the award recipient give the speech. So I got up in front of five hundred people in the audience and shouted, "Ladies and gentlemen, boys and girls, . . . stand back nonbelievers!" Then I told the TicketCity story. Was I nervous? Sure! But did I let that stop me from grabbing the spotlight? No way!

I follow the advice of Dr. Seuss: "Be who you are and say what you feel, because those who mind don't matter and those who matter don't mind." Don't be afraid to dive in and take some chances. Don't be afraid to go out on a limb. Don't be afraid to be spontaneous. "Think Different" as those Apple ads from way back encouraged.

Look at people like Sir Richard Branson, the British entrepreneur who founded the Virgin Records dynasty. He's a guy who's passionate and charismatic. He's someone who is obviously celebrating life and experiencing everything life has to offer. As he says himself, "Sometimes I do wake up in the mornings and feel like I've just had the most incredible dream. I've just dreamt my life." Now you're probably not a billionaire or business mogul, but that shouldn't keep you from dreaming big and living large!

When you put yourself out there, you give yourself the opportunity to be noticed and to make a difference. In my opinion, you can't take advantage of all the wonders life has to offer if you're not front and center. I always tell my kids that if they want to make an impact, they need to be the one head that truly stands out above the sea of heads. If you're nervous or shy about standing out in the crowd, feel the fear and do it anyway!

Seize the day and seize the moment. Maintain a positive outlook. Sure, we've all got to go through life's little trials and tribulations, whether we're waiting in a long line at the grocery store or sitting in traffic. You can get all worked up and stressed out, or you can use those times as opportunities to practice patience and positivity.

I remember having a meeting with one of my coaches and mentors. I got tied up on a call, so he had to wait in our lobby. As soon as I got off the call, I rushed out to the lobby and apologized. I said, "I'm so sorry for making you wait." He just smiled and said, "You weren't making me wait. I was enjoying the moment." Sure, he could have been checking his watch and getting frustrated because I was delayed, but instead he took the "cup half full" approach and made the most of a few quiet minutes. He was just savoring a "Zen moment" of peace and serenity—a moment of mindfulness!

FIND CLARITY

Sometimes it's tough to find clarity. There are times when I just can't figure things out, or I get stuck on something. I call this "founder's block." Maybe I'm too close to a situation or I just can't wrap my mind around a solution. I spent more than a year trying to figure out a future direction for the company. I thought I wanted to find a new CEO to replace myself at some point, but I couldn't quite sort it out.

Finally, after more than a year of sorting through resumes, interviewing candidates, and meeting with advisors, I finally saw the light and gained clarity. I realized the right person for the job was homegrown. He was right there under my nose, and he deserved a chance. I took my VP of marketing and moved him into the Chief Operating Officer role. Now he has taken over many of my CEO responsibilities and is thriving. I realized that patience is extremely important, and sometimes you need to take your time on important decisions in order to eventually speed up. Soon after, I was meeting with a colleague of mine, telling him about my plans for the company and my vision for TicketCity's future. He said, "Randy, that's the first time in over a year that I've seen you with clarity on what you want to do." I finally was clear about which direction we had to go. Sometimes it just takes some laser-like focus to clear your head.

In fact, we use several tools to help structure our thinking and align management at TicketCity. One tool is the simple 2 x 2 box. This is a four-quadrant square that helps us organize and structure our thinking. We list the projects we have to do first in the top right quadrant, the projects we will do in our spare time in the bottom right quadrant, the projects we will selectively invest in the top left quadrant, and the projects we will ignore in the bottom left quadrant. This enables us to prioritize our projects and focus our energy on what is most important for our company.

You can't be all over the board if you want to be successful. You need to slow down and focus. Sometimes you may need to walk away to clear your head. Do something completely different. Give yourself a change of scenery. Then come back and refocus on your project.

THE WORLD CUP

While soccer may not be the most popular spectator sport in the United States, the World Cup, the preeminent soccer tournament held every four years, is the most-watched sporting event in the world. The final game of the 2006 World Cup drew more than 700 million viewers.

TicketCity has been offering World Cup experiences for years, and passionate fans have spent as much as $8,000 for a championship ticket in one of the best seats. Order early at TicketCity.com because tickets go fast.

CELEBRATE WITH SPONTANEITY

Spontaneity is great for creating some fun times, and I'm spontaneous to a fault! Last weekend, at the spur of a moment, I flew out to surprise my dad in Florida. We went deep-sea fishing and spent a wonderful day together. It didn't take a lot of planning—I just decided to up and go. Some might call it impulsive; I call it spontaneously making life fun! Being unpredictable is a great way to get "unstuck." It's one of the ways I maintain clarity and overcome "founder's block".

Being spontaneous breaks up your routine, and keeps life interesting and unpredictable. Think about the expression on someone's face the last time you gave him or flowers. It's that unexpected surprise—the sheer delight that comes with a spontaneous show of appreciation.

Doing things on the spur of the moment also helps you keep things fresh and playful. Taking your office or your department out for an ice cream on a hot summer day is one example. Bringing home a little "today" present or treat for your kids for no particular reason is another. When I was a child my father used to surprise us with animals he would find on the way home from work. He brought home box turtles, garden snakes, and one time he even brought home a pet chicken! I would always race to the door with excitement and anticipation knowing that he might bring home a surprise.

Do something new. Try a new place for lunch. Take the scenic route home from work. Mix it up! Call an old friend to catch up. Schedule an impromptu getaway for you and your spouse or family. There are dozens of ways to keep life interesting and diverse! Just clear your head and then you can make room for these new and fresh ideas.

It's not always easy to be spontaneous or upbeat. Sometimes the world will try to drag you down. Maybe you're not getting enough rest, or you are frustrated by paying way too much for gas or for not getting great service at the drive-through line. Once again, it's mind over matter. You can stay positive if you keep things in perspective. Don't let life's little aggravations get you down. Lighten up! Think about how good you have it.

Wake up deciding that it's going to be a great day! Feel the water refresh you in the shower; smell the soap—use all your senses to wake up and come alive! Take a moment to appreciate all the good things in your life. Visualize a great day ahead of you, and then make it happen.

MAKE YOUR OFFICE YOUR INSPIRATION

To help me make sure that I'm living life to the fullest and maintaining a positive attitude, I create the right environment at work. My office inspires me. I've made it a priority to make my office a place that reminds me that life is good, life is exciting, and life is an adventure!

As I look around my office, I see all kinds of pictures of my children, including one with my kids and me standing next to a 250-pound blue marlin I caught when I was fishing in the waters off Cabo San Lucas. I have framed photos from incredible events, like the Olympics and the Kentucky Derby. I've got a big key to the city of Austin that was presented to me by Mayor Will Wynn. (By the way, the only other people I know of who have received a key to the city are Vicente Fox, the former president of Mexico, and the Dalai Lama, so I'm very humbled to be in such amazing company.)

I've got *Speed Racer* memorabilia to remind me that life moves fast. I've got a giant Dr. Seuss character—the Green-Lidded Fawn—sticking out of my wall like a mounted deer head trophy. On another wall is a map of the United States, showing the hundreds of locations where TicketCity invests in tickets. I also have framed copies of articles about the company.

The walls of my office at TicketCity are also adorned with original Disney animation cells from the 1930s and '40s. One of them shows a papa wolf leading three little wolves off to find adventure. I love it because it makes me think of me leading my kids to find fun. The other animation cell depicts three little ducklings checking out a cricket. That's a bit like my kids trying to figure out their crazy dad!

I even have the old children's toy Rock 'Em, Sock 'Em Robots set up on my desk. You may remember this game from when you were a kid. It's the one with the red and blue robots in the boxing ring, and you have to knock the opponent's block off! Sometimes we play this game right on my desk to settle arguments—it's just a way to remain playful and fun.

All these special things keep me motivated and upbeat because they surround me with memories of all the wonderful things in my life. But it's not just trophies and awards and photos from the past. I also use my environment to inspire me about the future. For example, on my desk I've got a couple of car models. One is a 1967 Shelby Mustang convertible; the other is a BMW Z8. I look at these models every day, and it helps me visualize and realize that one of these days I will get the real things.

Finally, I have items in my office and on my desk that help me remain constantly aware of my core values. Whether it's reminders on my computer screen saver or the sign on my desk that simply reads "Integrity," these things are frequent reminders to stay on track and live life right.

Do your home and office inspire you? What kind of environment have you created? Are you surrounded by things that motivate you to pursue your dreams? Try to make your environment conducive to success. Put yourself in surroundings that inspire and motivate you. Give yourself frequent reminders that life is great!

LEARN AND GROW

Another way to be sure you're seizing life's many opportunities is to continue to learn and grow. Never stop learning! A dear friend of mine, Rick Sapio, is a great example of someone who's constantly learning and evolving. His great success is due in large measure to his insatiable appetite for knowledge.

Rick goes out of his way to learn and discover new things, and he surrounds himself with fascinating, successful people. He recently spent five days for the second year in a row with Sir Richard Branson on Branson's private island with ten other CEOs, listening, learning, and playing. Rick loves to hang out and learn from billionaires. He's had lunch or dinner with half a dozen billionaires this year alone. How does he do it? He attends silent auctions and other charity events where the charity is giving away a chance to have lunch with a billionaire. Then he makes sure he bids high enough to win the opportunity to hang out with the high-powered bigwig.

You can learn so much from others, just like Rick does. You can learn through your own experiences, and you can even learn from your kids! As an entrepreneur, I believe in learning "on someone else's dime." In other words, learn while you earn: if you're working for someone else, you've got to take advantage of the opportunities to learn new things and develop new skills. It's like you're being paid to learn!

When I first got out of college, I started working for Wallace Computer Services. I was learning all about business, but I was getting paid at the same time. When I left to start my own company, I took with me many of those skills I learned on the job. Like the old saying goes, experience is the best teacher! Keep learning, keep improving, and keep your mind open to new ideas and knowledge! Never be foolish enough to think that you know it all; stay open to new possibilities.

CHOOSE LIFE!

To fully celebrate life, we must take advantage of the greatest gift known to humankind. It's what separates us from every other living being on the planet. It's so simple that we take it for granted. That gift is the power of choice.

We are blessed with freedom to choose. We get to decide who we are, what we do, where we live, and how we live. Aside from the family you're born into, you can make conscious decisions about nearly every aspect of your life. This is an awesome power that so few of us realize and appreciate!

One of the toughest business choices I've made was in 2000. In that year, I leveraged TicketCity by spending all of our cash—$250,000—to buy the Connecticut-based company SoldOut.com. My leadership team urged caution and did their due diligence. SoldOut.com was going bankrupt, and this purchase would give TicketCity our first major presence in the Northeast. Banks promised us the loan but could not come through in time, so we did it ourselves. This purchase was tremendous. Soon after, the Yankees and Mets made it into the World Series, and the Giants made it into the Super Bowl. Our new asset paid off within six months, and we still profit from it today.

It's easy to be a "Monday morning quarterback" with the wisdom of hindsight As I think about the past years, I know I've made some poor choices regarding employee retention. TicketCity has a great track record of keeping employees, but as I look back, I realize I let go employees who were passionate about their work and good at what they did. I wish now that I had worked through our differences and enabled those employees to blossom more under my guidance. It's kind of like Google's 80-20 rule. Google employees are allowed one day a week to work on whatever they choose, and amazing things have come from these creative individuals. I should have been able to work through my differences with my employees by providing them more freedom or more money or whatever! It is so important to make sure you keep your best players. Work at it. Where there is a will there is a way.

The power of choice means that we can determine our own destiny. We can make intentional plans and take action to shape our own lives—in whatever ways we want! As long as you've got this "super power," why not use it wisely? Make the choice to celebrate life. Decide to live life to the fullest. Choose happiness! It's all up to you! Remember those words of wisdom from President Lincoln: "A person is about as happy as he makes up his mind to be."

AMAZING PROFILES: SAM GOODNER

Throughout this book, we'll be sharing some profiles of amazing entrepreneurs. One such visionary leader is Sam Goodner, founder and CEO of Catapult Systems. Catapult Systems is a Microsoft-focused tech consulting firm that provides application development, enterprise solutions, and infrastructure services to their clients across the globe.

Sam started up Catapult Systems in 1993 at the ripe old age of twenty-six. Prior to founding Catapult, Sam ran the European operation for Service Systems International. He also developed software applications for Dell Computer Corporation's international offices.

Sam holds a B.S. in Computer Science from Texas A&M University, and like me, he's a graduate of the MIT/*Inc.* "Birthing of Giants" program. What's even more fascinating about Sam's background is that he was a mountain infantry officer in the Swiss Army!

Sam personifies many of the leadership tenets I espouse in this book, and he's built a great company on many of the same principles we practice at TicketCity. Sam says—and I heartily agree—that the key to success is employee empowerment. Not unlike TicketCity, Catapult puts a huge emphasis on corporate culture and employee empowerment. Sam's company has been recognized as the number one best place to work in Austin and been named the number two best company to work for in all of Texas.

When Sam Goodner says that Catapult is its people, it's more than just a corporate line. He really walks the walk by supporting his employees with mentoring, training, development, and plenty of opportunities for advancement. Goodner understands that people have lives outside the office, and Catapult promotes a healthy work/life balance.

Another reason I respect Sam and his company so much is because they practice what they preach: Catapult lives and breathes its core values. Catapult's values are the foundation of their business philosophies. Those values are woven into every aspect of the company from awards and celebrations to performance reviews and promotions. In fact, Catapult will not hire a new employee—no matter how qualified she is—unless her personal and professional standards match Catapult's core values.

What are those essential, core values? I've listed them here, since we could all take a page directly from Sam's playbook to improve our own companies:

- Accountability: Accept responsibility and take ownership. Do what you say you're going to do.
- Passion: Love what you do. Show enthusiasm in relation to work.

- Initiative: Be proactive. Make it happen. Innovate.
- Teamwork: Work together. Assist others. Share information.
- Agility: Adapt and respond quickly. Embrace change.
- Fun: Maintain a positive attitude. Contribute to a fun work environment

Sam's staff can make critical business decisions without having to ask for management approval. You can imagine how this streamlines operations and makes the company more nimble. Here's what Catapult expects their employees to ask themselves when faced with an on-the-spot decision or a new idea to improve a work process:

1. Is it right for the customer?
2. Is it right for Catapult Systems?
3. Is it ethical?
4. Is it in line with Catapult's core values?
5. Are you willing to be held personally accountable for your decision?

If the answer to all five questions is "yes," employees don't ask, they just do it.

Finally, Sam and his company are serious about their mission, or what they call their "brand promise." I think every growing company should develop a similar statement. Catapult's is simple, client-focused, and direct:

We Always Deliver. We are passionate about delivering on our commitments and doing what's right for you. Our most fundamental core value is that we do what we say we are going to do—always. Even when circumstances change or an unexpected situation arises, we will do whatever it takes to make it right for you.

We're Easy to Work With. We are committed to being the easiest, most flexible, and most convenient technology partner you have ever worked with. Our local, professional, and friendly employees go out of their way to respond quickly and accommodate your needs. We collaborate with your internal staff and other strategic partners and believe that long-term success is achieved through mutual education and information sharing.

We Bring the Whole Team. We do everything as a united Catapult team. Even when you engage a single consultant, you benefit from the collective experience, expertise, and creativity of our entire organization. When any one of our employees encounters a challenge, he has all our internal and external resources at his disposal to overcome it quickly. We have staked our reputation on hiring and retaining the most talented individuals in our industry, as well as partnering with the right firms to provide the most value to you.

Now that sounds like a company I'd like to do business with!

RULE #3
PUT FAMILY FIRST.

The only rock I know that stays steady, the only institution I know that works, is the family.
—*Lee Iacocca*

IF YOU WANT TO BE TRULY SUCCESSFUL in life, you've got to strive toward balance. Balance is that key ingredient that keeps you grounded and moving in the right direction. Too many successful executives have sacrificed their family lives in their climbs to the top of the corporate ladder. It's a familiar scenario: a person is wildly successful in one area of his life, but his family life is in shambles.

I made that mistake once, and it cost me a marriage. When I started TicketCity, I was so passionate about building a successful company that I lost sight of other truly important things, like my relationship with my family. The company was only four years old, and I was working sixteen-hour days even though I was newly married. After we had twins, I did an even worse job of balancing work and family. I didn't understand that in order to be successful at marriage and raising a family, you have to spend time with your family—to be present. I was not doing that, and my relationship failed. The good news is my ex-wife and I get along great today, and I spend more time than ever with my children.

I'm not willing to make that poor sacrifice of work over family again, and I'll bet that you're not either. I realized that for me, there's nothing more important than family. Family comes first; it's as simple as that. My feelings about family are summed up in this great quote from Desmond Tutu: "You don't choose your family. They are God's gift to you, as you are to them."

How can you ensure you don't make the same mistake I did? You make time for the things that are important to you. You prioritize. You plan your work, and you work your plan. I call this "time and territory management." It takes some setting of boundaries and some discipline, but it's a great way to achieve balance in your life.

I enjoy my work, so I could stay at the office until midnight every night and be content. However, balancing my family life is important to me, so I'm not going to work late every night. I set work limits for myself to ensure I make time for my children.

It's not always easy balancing the demands of work and family. Recently, my seven-year-old daughter had a special morning school event. That day was going to be my last day in the office before I took a big trip, so I was anxious to get to the office to take care of some business. But when I thought of my daughter doing her presentation without her dad there supporting her, it was a no-brainer to postpone going into work until after her event. I'm glad I was there for her, and I know she'll remember and appreciate that her dad took time out to see her that morning.

YOUR "DON'T-DO" LIST

I've got a to-do list, but I've also got a "don't-do" list! I believe that what you *don't* do is just as important as what you *do* do. At some point, you've got to decide what you're *not* going to do—what you're going to let go of so that you'll have time for the more important things. We live in a world of tough choices, and you have to determine what's not going to make the cut on your to-do list. The word *no* is empowering. It puts you in control and allows you to prioritize and choose the things that are most important.

Your "don't-do" list consists of those things that you've got to eliminate. Maybe you're not going to have time for a particular obligation, or you've got to choose which event to attend among three charity dinner invitations, or you're going to commit to *not* watch the new season of *American Idol*. Whatever it is, you remove it from your priorities to make time for the things that matter more to you.

One of the tools I use to prioritize my life is "performance journaling," a self-assessment technique to help keep me on track with certain goals and values. For example, one of my core values is being a good parent and making time for family. So I write that down and journal to get some clarity to see ways I can do that; then I take deliberate steps to execute that value.

To explain performance journaling further, I believe it is easy to figure things out when you can visualize them in front of you. I may performance journal every day, once a week, or maybe just monthly, depending on what challenging incident I am trying to work through. Here are the performance journaling steps I follow:

1. Write down the basic facts of the challenging incident: what happened?
2. Write down the context in which the incident occurred.
3. Write down my emotional state.
4. Write down my thoughts, beliefs, and assumptions from the incident.
5. Write down the implications or consequences that occurred from the incident.
6. Describe what I may have learned from the incident.
7. Make sure that I take what I learned to better handle future situations.

Performance journaling of an event allows you to self-improve so you can do a better job the next time a similar event happens. I compare it to the way Tiger Woods reviews his game film. The next time he is in a similar situation, he is prepared to tackle the problem to get the optimal outcome.

The other day I was sitting on the couch with my fourteen-year-old twin boys, and I realized that the three of us were just sitting on our butts, "vegging out." I thought back to my performance journaling—my tracking tool—and realized that this wasn't exactly quality family time. So I got off my butt and asked my sons if they wanted to go fishing. We went down to the lake and caught some bass. Then we decided to play some b-ball and shoot baskets. Instead of wasting time staring at the TV, we did some fun things as a family and had great quality time together. I want to be a great dad, but I realize that takes a conscious effort.

If you want to balance your family life with your work life, I suggest you make your own to-do and don't-do lists to help you decide how you're going to make room for the essential things in your life. Put family first! Don't wake up one day and find that your kids are grown and those precious years are gone forever. You don't want to end up like the dad who has no time for his son and later comes to regret it in that Harry Chapin song "Cat's in the Cradle."

LISTEN UP

Make your family time count: Be there for your kids—and listen to them. I grew up in a wonderful Jewish home, and we definitely weren't shy! But everyone was busy, so we didn't spend that much time together as a family—time where we sat down and really talked and listened to each other. That is one of the reasons I believe family time is so important to me now. My sisters, Tammy and Rachel, and I were involved in a lot of sports and activities, so we were always on the go, racing from activity to activity: off to school, rush home, go to practice, chow down Hamburger Helper, then do homework. We rarely slowed down to connect. So I make the effort to listen to my kids, and believe me, it is an effort! I've discovered you can get your kids to open up to you if you really engage them and listen. Take an interest and let them know that what they have to say is important to you. (This is good advice for working with your employees, as well!)

I certainly can't claim to be the world's greatest parent just yet, but I'm trying to be! My kids get into a little mischief now and then. Sometimes, I want to secretly laugh at some of the things they do, but I know I have to be the parent and set the boundaries. As you know, there's no instruction manual for raising kids. And what worked last month isn't necessarily going to work this month!

I'm not always sure how to discipline my kids. Most of the time, there are a hundred different paths I could take. But I'm a big fan of setting goals and incentives for the kids. Here's where listening closely and paying attention to what's important to your kids can help you. What do your children—or your employees, for that matter—get excited about? What motivates them? If you can find out what is special to them, what they really value, you can set up incentives for good behavior.

I played soccer as a kid, and my coach was John Cooke, the son of the legendary owner of the Washington Redskins football team, Jack Kent Cooke. It was pretty amazing to have the son of this remarkable sports entrepreneur coaching our team. But what impressed me even more at the time was that Jack offered incentives to the kids on our team. One time, our coach told us that whoever practiced the hardest that week would get to be Jack's guest at a Washington Redskins game. Now that was a powerful incentive for me! I was a huge Redskins fans, and I had never been to a pro football game, let alone a Redskins game with the owner of the team!

As you can imagine, I practiced my heart out that week. I made sure the coach saw me working harder, running faster, giving more, and digging in to make that extra effort. I was motivated. I had incentive. I was going to do whatever it took to get to that game. Guess what? I practiced the hardest that week and won the right to go to the Redskins game that Sunday. It was incredible!

MY WORK FAMILY

I've got a relatively small team of employees, and many of them have been with me and TicketCity for a long time. We've got a lot of history together: we've been through good times and bad. That probably makes it easier for me to think of my employees as family, but I've still got to work at it, month after month, year after year. In fact, everyone on our staff works hard to maintain a close family atmosphere.

From the top on down, TicketCity makes a concerted effort to promote a positive, supportive working environment. This starts with your genuine interest and concern regarding the lives of your employees, but it's also the little things you do that show you care. For example, we have a party on the first day of work for each new employee. Doesn't it make better sense to have a welcome party, rather than a farewell party on an employee's last day?

When a new employee walks in the door at TicketCity, he or she is greeted by the entire staff. The new hire gets balloons and cake and plenty of camaraderie. Then that new team member can go home at the end of that first day and tell her spouse, partner, mom, or friends that TicketCity had a party in her honor! It wasn't just a run-of-the-mill first day at the office.

We try to do the little things that make a big difference—that build and foster family spirit. We'll have breakfast tacos for the staff some mornings, or we'll host a happy hour after work. We often buy lunch for the entire office during chaotic crunch times. I have a sign-up sheet outside my office so employees can sign up for "lunch with da boss" anytime they want. Sometimes at lunchtime, I'll just yank someone away from work so that each employee gets one-on-one time with me, and I get to know what's going on in each person's life. I like to keep up with what is important to my team.

When someone in our work family has a birthday, I call them up—even if I'm on the road—and sing "Happy Birthday" to them! And I sing it *my way*. It may not be the best rendition they'll ever hear, but they will definitely remember it. There are plenty of companies that talk about their staffs being a family, but we *live* it. You've got to live it and breathe it to mean it. TicketCity has been named one of the "Best Places to Work" in Austin several times, and nothing makes me more proud!

Of course, there are good business reasons why it makes sense to keep your staff happy. Productivity studies have indicated that a company can get up to five times more effort from employees when morale is high. If people feel like they're part of a family at work, and if they're having fun and enjoying their work, that's going to be reflected in how your business performs. That's why I'm always insisting that you do what you love and love what you do! Happy employees translate to happy customers! And happy customers equal good business.

Each day we work hard to make a difference for all our clients, but we also believe in enjoying life with our families and friends. In addition, it's also important that we participate in various events around town and give back to our community. The fun, collaborative culture we've created here also demonstrates to our customers that there are real people behind TicketCity.

OUR COMPANY CULTURE

A business is a reflection of the people who work for it, and TicketCity represents the passion and knowledge of our employees. Our business may be selling tickets, but what we really provide is access to great experiences— the kind you want to attend so that you can feel the range of emotions that makes them so unforgettable. We understand the joy that comes from those experiences because we are fans of these events and attend them just like our customers do.

When Rick, one of my sales guys, was working the Kentucky Derby, he wanted to find one of his customers he had sold tickets to. Now Rick had never met this customer in person, but he knew where the customer's seats were and figured he'd recognize the guy's voice. So Rick walked over and introduced himself. The client could not have been more excited to meet Rick! The client immediately said, "Hey, this is the guy I was telling you about! This is Rick from TicketCity who got all these great seats for us! This is the guy who made all this happen!"

That's the kind of passion and customer evangelism that we strive for, and I think you can only get it by delivering excellent care and concern for the client. Rick is an example of someone who goes above and beyond when it comes to his clients. He cares, he communicates, and he "superserves" his customers. Rick is passionate about customer service, so his customers become raving fans. They become part of the larger TicketCity family!

PRESENCE, NOT PRESENTS

I believe the single greatest gift you can give to your family—whether it's your family at home or your work family—is your time. Not just face time, but real time. What I mean is that you've got to be present and in the moment. Being there for your family means really *being* there. One of the definitions of *being* is "conscious existence." We need to be conscious, awake, alive, and present when we are spending time with our loved ones.

Children especially need your *presence* more than your presents! As a divorced dad, I get to see my kids only "half" the time, so it's really important for me to be present when I'm with them. Often, that takes extra effort and planning so we don't end up just wasting time or staring blankly at the television. I love to do things with my family, so we plan activities and adventures and experiences. My hope is that, not unlike with my business family, we are creating memories that will last a lifetime!

Everyone seems to agree that time is the new commodity. We're all so overscheduled and crunched for time that time has become more precious than ever. Give your family the gift of your time, and they won't forget it. We've all heard the old expression that when we're on our deathbeds, we are certainly not going to wish we had spent more time at the office!

No one has ever died from too much loving. So give your family your time, your attention, and your full presence. Really listen to them. Find out what's important to them. You won't regret it! Treat these relationships as high-priority goals, and don't forget to focus on the little things, too. You can't let your family be an afterthought, or something you have time for only when your work obligations are done. These relationships need more nurturing and attention than all your other work and personal goals. The key to a harmonious family life can be summed up in a quote attributed to motivational speaker and author Zig Ziglar: "You can have everything in life that you want if you just give enough other people what they want."

Besides making time to connect and listen to your kids, it's important to teach them self-esteem. It's not easy to instill confidence in children, but you've got to make the effort to build them up. I always tell my kids to look a person in the eye when they're talking with someone and to speak up, be prepared, and act confident. I practice with them and role-play so they'll develop more self-assurance as they deal with other people.

I also want to lead by example to teach integrity—both at home and at the office. The only way to put real value in a business is to do the right thing and maintain high ethical standards. I have a sign on my desk that simply says "integrity." To me, that means being courageous, being clear and straight in your communications, and surrounding yourself with others who share those same values. It also means you need to give up being right all the time!

Remember that time is a precious commodity. So even if you can only give certain people little slivers of your time, that still means a lot. Take a few minutes to let someone know that you're thinking of him or her. Call your mom, for example. Or send her a note. Small, thoughtful gestures can make someone's day.

FRIENDS AND FAMILY

For me, it all comes back to friends and family. These relationships are what make life worth living. Chances are, the better your relationships are, the more successful you're going to be in every aspect of life. I think back to that line from *It's a Wonderful Life*: "No man is a failure who has friends."

I also look for the "amazing" in my friends. I'm blessed with wonderful friendships, and I believe part of the reason that is true is that I look for and try to bring out the best in people. I like people who are upbeat, passionate, and genuine. Many of the success gurus out there will tell you that you're only going to be as successful as the five people you spend the most time with, so I choose my friends carefully!

We often feed off the energy and emotion of our friends, so I try to surround myself with enthusiastic and passionate people. By the same token, you've got to give people a chance. Find that spark or glimmer in them. Give them an opportunity to shine and to show you what is special or unique about them. Everyone has something to offer if you're willing to look for it and "find the amazing." (See the next chapter for more about finding the amazing.)

AMAZING PROFILES: WILL MUSCHAMP

If you're the highest-paid assistant coach in college football's Big 12 Conference, you must be pretty amazing! Especially when that top salary doubled in 2009. Longhorn Defensive Coordinator Will Muschamp is so amazing, he is already slated to succeed Mack Brown as the head football coach for the University of Texas when Brown eventually retires.

As an undergraduate, Muschamp attended the University of Georgia, where he played safety for the Bulldogs. He was the defensive cocaptain his senior season and appeared in two bowl games while at Georgia. Teammates described Will as a hard worker who was very physical and intense. As a coach, Muschamp has gained a reputation for his excellent defenses as well as his fiery demeanor on the field.

Despite Muschamp's young age, the thirty-seven-year-old Georgia native has had an excellent coaching career, beginning at Auburn in 1995, where he was a graduate assistant coach while he earned his Master of Education degree.

In 2001, Muschamp joined Nick Saban's coaching staff as the linebacker coach at LSU. The following year, he became the defensive coordinator there, and in 2003, LSU won the BCS national football championship, with Muschamp's defense leading the nation in both scoring defense and total defense.

Muschamp went on to spend a season as the assistant head coach for defense for the NFL's Miami Dolphins before returning to college ball at Auburn. In his second year at Auburn, Muschamp was a finalist for the 2007 Broyles Award for the most outstanding coach in college football.

In January 2008, Muschamp became the defensive coordinator for the University of Texas Longhorns, a team nationally ranked in the top three. Before the end of the 2008 season, UT announced that Muschamp would take over the head coaching job when Mack Brown eventually steps down. Though that may be a while, Muschamp says, "This is a special place. I think it's *the* elite job in the country."

Muschamp's intensity and passion have made him popular with players, fans, and management alike. For Texas and for Muschamp, that passion has paid off.

ENERGY

RULE #4
TAKE CARE OF YOUR PEOPLE. FIND THE AMAZING.

As we look ahead into the next century, leaders will be those who empower others.
—*Bill Gates*

WATCHING THE INDY 500 is always a fantastic experience, but in 2005 the excitement was over the top. In that year, Danica Patrick exploded onto the scene as a twenty-one-year-old shining star. She nearly took pole, and she became the first female driver to lead the race en route to a fourth-place finish. It was the best finish by a woman at Indy, and it helped her take Rookie of the Year honors. Although she placed fourth, Patrick definitely stole the show from Dan Wheldon, the Englishman who won the race. And Patrick continued to be in the spotlight as the press hounded her, asking when she would actually win an IndyCar Series race.

Next question, please.

Patrick, competing in her fiftieth IndyCar Series race, became the first female to win a major auto-racing event on a closed-course circuit. She won the Indy Japan 300 on April 20, 2008.

As we have seen so many times in sports, people who seem ordinary can do extraordinary things. They just have to be treated right. One of the most gratifying things about building my company over the years is that we've been included in several "best places to work" lists. We're fortunate that we've been able to build a culture that supports one another. Everyone on our team is dedicated, passionate, and happy to be at TicketCity. That's one of the secrets to our success, and it's the reason we've got such longevity among our staff. There's very little turnover, and the entire management team has been with me since the early days.

I'll admit that having such loyalty and stability is a source of great pride. As a rapidly growing business, it's an enviable position to be in. But it's no accident. We work hard to create a culture of passion and camaraderie, and we nurture and empower our staff.

We develop this culture by "finding the amazing." Simply put, I try to find the best in people. I discover what they're good at, and then I bring out their natural talents and abilities and give them a chance to shine. What are their passions? What is special about them? What lights them up? How can they best use their unique skills?

Not unlike a great football coach or scout, you've got to identify that talent early on and then find out how best to develop those raw materials and abilities. You may see a little something in someone—some kind of spark, a glimmer of potential. Then you've got to nurture that nugget, cultivate it. It may take years to develop, but it's worth the time and effort.

Back in the 2000 NFL draft, someone in the New England Patriots organization saw something special in a young kid from San Mateo, California. As a football player at the University of Michigan, that kid had been seventh on the depth chart, not seeing much playing time until his junior year. That's when he began to shine.

Still, as an NFL draft prospect, he was mostly flying under the radar. The kid was a sixth-round draft pick and the 199th pick overall. As a rookie with the Patriots, he was the fourth-string quarterback. But he worked his way up to become starter Drew Bledsoe's backup, and he took over for an injured Bledsoe in a game against the Jets on September 21, 2001. The rest, as they say, is history. Of course, I'm talking about Tom Brady, the 199th draft pick who has become one of the best NFL quarterbacks in the game. In fact, the NFL network even named Brady the greatest draft "steal" of all time.

Perhaps you've got a Tom Brady in your company waiting to be discovered and given a chance. Everyone has something special to offer if you just take the time to uncover it. With some prospects this may take some digging—but you've got to find the amazing in that individual. There's an old proverb that says, "Friendship is a plant that must be watered often." I would argue that employees, too, are plants that need water!

You've got to look for that glimmer—it could be something as simple as a genuine smile. When I'm scouting new talent, I look for people who are passionate and have heart. I want people who can put themselves out there. I want people who believe in themselves and aren't afraid to discuss, debate, and go out on a limb. I want people who can give the credit, take the blame, and always show compassion.

If you want to nurture that kind of talent, I suggest that you take the time to find out what your employees are good at. Boost them up. Encourage them, find out what their values are, and help them along. Give them the opportunity to maximize their potential and discover their gifts.

TAKE CARE OF YOUR PEOPLE

TicketCity has been blessed with a wonderful, long-lasting staff—some team members have been with me since I started the company in 1990! That kind of loyalty and longevity is a direct result of how we treat our people. We take care of our employees and treat them as well as we treat our customers.

We've truly been able to build a family here, and I'd encourage anyone who can create that kind of environment to do so. If you take good care of your people, the payoff will be huge. We empower and enable our people— we challenge them. We treat our staff like family because we *are* a family!

Still, it goes way beyond employee summer picnics or holiday staff parties. It's about opportunities, involvement, and empowerment. It's about creating a team environment from top to bottom. It's about sharing the burdens and sharing the rewards. We set goals and we involve everyone. We have an open-book philosophy and a big board that shows our numbers. Everything is out in the open, and everyone in the company has access. So if we hit our targets and make our quarterly numbers, *everyone* in the company splits a huge bonus. Every single employee shares in the rewards. It may be a cliché, but it works for us: All for one and one for all.

Like any team sport, we share a common goal of victory. We pull together during good times and bad. In fact, when things have been the bleakest at TicketCity, my team has always stepped up, figured things out, and made it happen. That dedication is rewarded not only monetarily but also with opportunities for continued growth, development, and education. I don't want my team to ever stop learning, so we encourage educational opportunities. We challenge our people to take risks, try new things, and not be afraid to screw up. If you're not going to put that kind of energy and enthusiasm in your work, you might as well work on an assembly line or in a job that doesn't really require you to think.

We want people who are excited to come to work: people who have passion and purpose. That's the kind of energy we share here—and it's contagious! We have fun, we bring our A-game, we stick together, and we succeed together. I think that's why we've had such team loyalty and so little turnover over the years. Everyone is happy to be here, and they're excited to be part of the TicketCity family. If you can create a culture that everyone wants to be a part of, you're on your way to becoming a great company.

Of course, when you're talking about great places to work, Google certainly comes to mind! Google's reputation for fostering a fun and creative workplace is legendary. From the amazing, free healthy meals served at the company café to the playful atmosphere that infuses the campus, it's easy to see why the "Googleplex" is known as *the* place to work in Silicon Valley.

As former Google head chef and "minister of cultural affairs" Charlie Ayers told David Vise, the author of *The Google Story*, "There was electricity in the air. Everyone was on fire. As soon as you walked in, you were hit with this onslaught of color. Vibrant colors in the lobby, lava lamps, people riding around on scooters in the hallways, things you didn't see anywhere else."

Google may be an extreme example of putting fun and heart into your business, but it is possible to create that kind of culture if you take great care of your people and you do all the little things that create a positive work environment.

BRINGING OUT THE BEST

How do you find the amazing in people? You spend time with them. You pay attention. You watch how they interact with customers and their peers. You communicate with them. I always make time for my team, from top to bottom. How else can you build relationships and discover strengths? I take my team members to lunch, have one-on-one meetings, and acknowledge their good work. It's too easy to take people for granted—so I really make the effort to understand everything they have to offer.

I find that if I give someone a chance to step up, he or she is usually going to seize the opportunity and pleasantly surprise me. If that employee knows that I care about her—that I've taken the time to find out what's important—she is going to go the extra mile for me. She is going to work a little smarter.

As I said, I'm looking for people with heart. People who are trustworthy—people who are believable, have credible voices, and are willing to meet things head on. Most of the actual job functions can be taught, but passion and heart come from within.

Does it take time to find the amazing? Of course. Is it more challenging as a manager to keep track of birthdays and anniversaries and what matters to people? Sure it is, but it's worth it! Spend time with your team. Find out what excites or motivates them. Do they want a raise, or extra vacation time? Maybe they're just looking for an opportunity to try something new. Communicate. Figure out what makes them tick, and then show that you care. When your team members recognize that you're looking out for them—that you go out of your way to take care of them—they are going to be passionate about their jobs and work harder for you.

When we have our monthly all-staff meetings, we'll name an employee of the month and hand that winner a crisp new one-hundred-dollar bill. There will be high fives and shout-outs and all kinds of accolades to individuals who excelled that month. Give those superstars their well-deserved moment in the sun.

Of course, we do happy hours and catered events and holiday parties, but we try to go beyond that and find new ways to work and play together. We're quick to reward hard work, and we offer plenty of chances for bonuses and incentives. Any company can have a summer staff picnic, but not many businesses can reward their employees by sending them to the Kentucky Derby or the U.S. Open!

Not only do we motivate and fire up our team members, but we give them the tools they need to succeed. We coach them. We invest in ongoing education. We keep everyone in the loop about what's going on inside the company. We have a lot of transparency, so every employee has access to the information about how we're doing and what our goals are. I believe in an open-book system; that way we're all on the same page.

I also have weekly one-on-one meetings with my managers, and the managers have one-on-ones with their direct reports. Those meetings give us the opportunity to communicate and ask, "What are the three biggest things that you are working on this week?" Then we hold each person accountable. And that accountability works both ways: employees can hold their managers accountable as well!

Accountability is a big deal at TicketCity. We see accountability not just as a way to track and measure our progress but also as a way to show our team that we care about what they're doing and that we want to empower them to succeed. If we weren't paying attention, or we didn't expect our employees to answer for their progress, they'd probably get the impression that we didn't really care. We not only care about their success, but we strive to find the amazing in all of them.

THE L-A-E-R MODEL

In order to find the amazing and seek out the good in people, you've got to be present with them. You've got to listen and observe. You've got to engage and be engaged. It's one thing to listen, but it's so much more powerful if the person you're talking with knows that they are being *heard*.

Research indicates that the average person living in or near a metropolitan area is bombarded with 3,500 marketing messages every day! That means that each person in those areas is exposed to 24,500 messages a week and over 1.2 million marketing messages each year! With all that noise, is it any wonder that we're distracted and have trouble listening?

That's why you can really make a difference with a person by focusing and truly listening. To help us do this we use the L-A-E-R model: *Listen. Acknowledge. Explore. Respond.* This process can be used to improve relationships at home or at the office.

The first step of the L-A-E-R model is to Listen. Most of the time we're so busy trying to think of what to say next that we're not listening to the other person. It's okay to pause, to leave a little silence in the exchange. It's too bad we are often uncomfortable with silence in a conversation. Take the time to think about what is being said, and then give yourself a moment to provide a thoughtful response.

If you truly listen and pay attention, it will be easy to Acknowledge what was said. We acknowledge by repeating back what someone says. This shows your dialogue partner that he or she has been heard. By acknowledging, you not only show a person the respect of listening to them, but you also give yourself more time to consider an appropriate response. If one of my sales staff is on the phone with a customer, for example, he will *listen* to the customer's initial request, and then *acknowledge* it by repeating the request back to the client: "So, you want four tickets to the Red Sox/Yankees game at Fenway Park on X date."

The third step of the L-A-E-R process is Explore. If we return to our Red Sox ticket request, my salesperson will explore and ask questions: "What's your budget? Where do you want to sit?" We'll dig a little deeper to find the exact needs of the customer. We'll explore whether the client wants tickets between home and third, home and first, or behind home plate to see the balls break. Ask questions. Be an investigator.

The last step of the model is Respond. You've done your homework, and you're ready to give your response: "Okay, Mr. King, you told me you want four tickets to the Red Sox/Yankees game at Fenway on X date, and you have a budget of $400 per ticket. I've got great tickets for you, and I recommend that you sit down the first-base line. I can get you in the field box area. Do you want to put that on your MasterCard or Visa?"

TEN SIMPLE WAYS TO FIND THE AMAZING IN YOUR EMPLOYEES

1. Ask questions—make an effort to get to know each person.
2. Observe—catch your team members doing things right.
3. Show an interest in their passions and hobbies.
4. Spend quality "one-on-one" time with them.
5. Have them share their proudest accomplishments with you.
6. Create opportunities for bonding, such as off-site retreats, staff dinners, etc.
7. On a similar note, participate in team-building exercises.
8. Explore their histories—discuss their childhoods and fond memories.
9. Find out their "why"—what is it that makes them get up every morning.
10. Ask who their heroes and mentors are; this will give you clues to their own attributes and aspirations.

Every one of my employees is taught the L-A-E-R process so that they can truly respond to a customer's request in an attentive and thoughtful manner. People aren't used to being heard, so it's a pleasant surprise for them when they realize they are being given 100 percent attention. Listening is definitely a lost art!

YOU'RE AMAZING, TOO!

Now that you've discovered some of the ways to find the amazing in others, let's be sure not to neglect one other amazing person: *you!* I'm sure you've heard it a thousand times, but the cliché is true: You can't love others until you love yourself. Put another way, if you want to be loved, you have to be lovable.

Success begins with self-respect and self-confidence. While we're busy finding the amazing in friends, family, and employees, we can't forget to reflect on our own strengths and find the best in ourselves. After all, if you don't believe that you're amazing, how do you expect others to find the amazing in you?

You've got unique gifts and talents, and you can be even more amazing by continuing to share those talents with the world. Think about all that you have to offer. Share your passions and your personality. Leave a little bit of you and your persona wherever you go. Try to be the type of person who lights up a room, who people are happy to see. Spread your optimism and positive vibe to others. Consider the oft-quoted saying: "Long after people remember what you've done, they will remember how you made them feel!"

FINDING THE AMAZING IN YOUR BUSINESS

When you look for the good in yourself and others, you're focusing on the positive aspects of those relationships. "Accentuate the positive and eliminate the negative!" I always say. It's easy to find the amazing when you're seeking out the best in people.

But can you find the amazing in your business? Is it possible to determine and emphasize the best attributes of your company? Of course it is! You can call it advertising or promotion, but focusing on what's great and special about your own company is just good business!

In fact, you've got to find the amazing in your company and let customers and partners know why they should do business with you. What makes your company special? What's unique about it? What is your company *great* at doing? Why should the customer choose you? Find those amazing things that separate your business and distinguish you from the competition. Those in the advertising industry call this your "unique selling proposition," or USP. But I call it good, old-fashioned "praisin' the amazin'." In other words, identify what's great about your company and let your customers know!

In the ticket business—and more than likely in your business, too—the competition is fierce, and the customer has dozens of options. Why should the customer choose you? Why should she spend her hard-earned money with you instead of the other guy? You've got to let each customer know exactly why you deserve her business. You must convince the potential buyer that you're more "amazing" than the next guy. Then you've got to prove it over and over again. Make that customer's experience with you so amazing that they'll keep coming back for more. Make a promise and keep that promise. It's as simple—and as difficult—as that.

As an example of finding (and promoting) the amazing in TicketCity, here's our promise to customers. You could call it our mission statement or our commitment to our clients. Whether it's a mantra or a manifesto, the following is one way we help our customers find the amazing when they buy from TicketCity.

THAT'S THE TICKET!

A BETTER EXPERIENCE LIVES HERE!

Our business may be selling tickets, but we're really about providing great *experiences*. The events we sell are ones that you will reminisce about with your friends for years to come. You'll encounter a range of emotions that make these events unforgettable.

We specialize in college sports and championship events tickets. College sports events are the best because they are full of passion. College fans are fiercely loyal to their schools, and those feelings are on display when you attend one of our great college games. The championship events we sell tickets to are the most prestigious events in the world. They are conversation starters and provide memories that you can share for the rest of your life. Here are five important points about our business:

1. **We want buying tickets from us to be as unforgettable as the events themselves.**

   - The reason for our success? We love what we do!
   - We are fans of the events we sell, just like our clients.
   - Attending the events we sell is an experience that will create lifelong memories.

2. **We have been in business since 1990 and have more than 250,000 loyal and happy customers.**

   - Our experience ensures that you get the best tickets available.
   - Our many years in business mean you can trust us with your business.

3. **We have the largest selection of college sports and championship events, ensuring that you get the seats you want.**

   - We own season tickets for more than 100 colleges.
   - We own a house down the street from the entrance to Augusta National.
   - We sell more Kentucky Derby tickets than anyone in the world!

4. **We let you talk directly to our college sports and championship events experts.**

   - We let you talk to real, live humans over the phone.
   - We have over 130 years of combined experience.
   - We attend the events, so we can tell you the things you need to know!

5. **We are so sure that we can get you the tickets you want that we offer an industry-best 200 percent guarantee.**

   - Our competitors' 100 percent guarantee only gives you back your money.
   - We deliver so consistently that we'll pay you if we are ever wrong.

FINDING THE AMAZING IN EVERY DAY

One way I'm able to maintain a wonderful, positive attitude in my business is by finding the amazing in every day. Each day always has something great to offer—it's just a matter of seeing it! Some motivational gurus might call this gratitude. To me, it's just my usual "woowoo" demeanor! It's great because it's contagious and it trickles down to others.

When I come to work fired up and excited, that energy spreads throughout the staff. I strive to find that passion and that exuberance every day. I do it by looking forward to learning something new or teaching something new on a daily basis. I'm having fun; I'm jazzed up about the day; I'm high-fiving people and having a good time. Some people might think I'm a little wacky, but I don't care. I'd much rather be fun than dull! Wouldn't you?

To me, life is all about a *wow*. Noticing what's going right and what's good about the day is how you find that wow. I want TicketCity to put the wow out there. We like wowing people! If you can't be a "wow" company, than why bother? I tell my friends who are unhappy in their jobs, "If you don't enjoy what you're doing, find something else to do!" If you hate your job, get the hell out and find something more fulfilling! Life's way too short for you to be miserable. You owe it to yourself and the people in your life to find your *wow*!

BEING AMAZING

It's great to know how far you can go with passion, optimism, and a great attitude. But what else do you need to be amazing?

If you're just starting out or have a new gig and you want to amaze your boss, you've got to show that drive and willingness to learn from day one. You've got to be willing to do whatever it takes. Dive in. Be enthusiastic. Be like the ball player who says, "Put me in, coach! I'll play outfield; I'll play third base—whatever you need, coach! Tell me what you need, and you got it!"

Remember, never quit! I don't care how tired you are, how much it hurts, how hard it is. Get back out there and go down swinging! When your teammates or business coworkers see you give it your all, they will reach down, too, and give you everything they've got!

So, especially as a newbie, your attitude has to be 100 percent all in. You've got to be the one saying, "I'm in. I'm on it. Sign me up!" This shows your dedication and the fact that you're willing to work long, hard hours and seize the opportunity to do whatever it takes to get the job done. That's how you get noticed. That's how you amaze.

One of the reasons that TicketCity has been so successful is that we've got an *amazing* team. We've been able to find the amazing in our people, but they've rewarded us by going all out and doing whatever it takes to get the job done. Our people go the extra mile and give us dedication and passion because we're all in this together. I'm down "in the trenches" with them doing the grunt work, and when it's time for fun and rewards, we bring the folks in the trenches up with us. Everyone is willing to do whatever it takes, regardless of titles, seniority, or history. Everyone pitches in and everyone shares in the spoils.

Obviously, it's a lot easier in a small, forty-five-person company like ours. However, whether you've got forty-five people or 45,000, the leaders have to lead by example. Employees will look to the top for their cues. They will know if you're doing the right thing. Set the example. Set the high standard. Set the tone. Your employees are looking to you for that model. Earn the trust and respect of your staff—across the board—and then don't betray that trust!

Remember, when you work to be an amazing boss, and you find the amazing in your people, you're on your way to forging a great company! To me, that's what leadership is all about.

AMAZING PROFILES: JON DANIELS

At first glance, you may not think that Jon Daniels is a baseball guy. He's thin, under six feet tall, and a bit on the nerdy side. In fact, he hasn't played the game since he was in the eighth grade. Daniels is the first to admit that his on-the-field skills were marginal. It's unlikely that he ever pondered a career in baseball.

Still, thirty-year-old Jon Daniels is now the general manager of the Texas Rangers and the youngest GM ever in major league baseball. He's never played a single pro inning of baseball, yet the slightly geeky Daniels has the power to trade $8 million-per-year ball players or fire managers who have been in the game much longer than he's been alive. Jon Daniels is the new "boy wonder," and he's one of an elite group of young GMs who are changing the game.

In his third season as general manager for the Rangers, Daniels is transforming the team's front office and cleaning up the messes he inherited from his predecessors. He's taking an overpriced roster and a weak farm system and building for the future. Daniels has made questionable moves that may yet prove brilliant. For example, he traded the Rangers' top pitching prospect, Edinson Volquez, to Cincinnati for outfielder Josh Hamilton. Not one to shy away from taking chances, Daniels still consulted with more than a dozen staffers before making the trade. To some, it seemed like a crazy move. After all, Hamilton is a reformed crack addict who had been written off by most. However, halfway through the 2008 season, Josh Hamilton led the league in RBIs (Runs Batted In). More impressive, the slugger belted a record-setting twenty-eight home runs in the first round of the 2008 All-Star Game's Home Run Derby. By taking a chance on Hamilton, Daniels may end up looking like a genius.

Daniels grew up a Mets fan in Queens, New York, but never dreamed of running a baseball team. He graduated from Cornell University with a degree in applied economics and management, and went to work for the parent company of Dunkin' Donuts and Baskin-Robbins ice cream. However, Daniels didn't love his job, and he jumped on an opportunity to do a six-month paid internship with the Colorado Rockies. All he had to do was leave his $40,000-a-year job for the $7,000 baseball internship.

So once he made that leap, Daniels made the most of it. He worked his tail off, learning everything he could during those six months. At the close of the internship, he interviewed with the Texas Rangers organization, which needed a baseball operations assistant. The Rangers were impressed, and Daniels got the gig. Then, just three years later, Jon Daniels was named general manager of the team. He was only a month over the age of twenty-eight.

Daniels's success is due in part to his collaborative style and his desire to create a culture where people are happy to work. He personifies many of the attributes we've discussed in this book: He takes chances, he tries to make it fun, and he has passion and energy.

"I want everyone's opinion," says Daniels. "A good leader knows his limitations and doesn't try to hide them." He trusts the people around him. In addition to taking input from his staff, Jon Daniels has shifted the culture of the Rangers organization, making it a much more employee-friendly place to work. "Things work better when people are happy to be here," concludes Daniels. These days, birthdays are acknowledged, Mother's Day cards are sent out, and employees receive thank-you notes with Starbucks gift cards enclosed.

His team-building goes beyond the staff to player development and scouting, an area where the Rangers had been notoriously weak. Rangers' scouts are instructed to go above and beyond in finding and courting new talent. Scouts are encouraged not only to file the typical reports but also to visit the homes of amateurs to get to know their families. Rangers' scouts even go to high school football games and track meets looking for potential talent. They use unique and unconventional ways to find young baseball prospects. As a result, their lackluster farm system has gone from being ranked twenty-eighth in the league to being ranked fourth.

Despite the fact that Jon Daniels has never been a baseball coach, it's clear that, as the youngest MLB general manager in history, Daniels understands the importance of coaching and being coached!

RULE #5
HAVE FUN. LEARN TO LAUGH!

People rarely succeed unless they have fun in what they are doing.
—Dale Carnegie

RICK RIVERA, WHO HAS BEEN WITH TICKETCITY for over eight years, went to his first Kentucky Derby last year and had a fabulous time, despite working twelve-hour days, taking care of clients, and buying and selling tickets. In the evenings he attended swanky parties to meet new clients. He went to the Oaks and the Derby and met celebrities and high-profile customers. Rick still talks about the amazing time he had, and he can't wait to go again.

I've said it before, but it bears repeating: Love what you do, do it well, and keep on doing it! You've gotta make work fun!

Find the fun in everything you do. That doesn't mean that everything you do is going to be a laugh a minute. No one expects you to have fun at the dentist or to enjoy waiting for a delayed flight at the airport or to smile while you're changing a flat tire. Those frustrations are inevitable. However, you can either make a conscious decision to let a nuisance ruin your day, or you can choose to make the best of it and move on. How you decide to react to the bumps in the road is completely up to you.

One thing's for sure: you're going to have a lot more fun in life if you view the glass as half full! After all, fun is really just a state of mind. It's maintaining a positive attitude. It's making the best of your situation and living in the moment. Having fun and being fun is your willingness to try new things—to stay open to new possibilities. Sometimes fun is just about being flexible or unselfish, and sometimes it's about being silly or spontaneous.

I love to have fun, and most folks will tell you that I'm a fun guy. Why? Well, as I've admitted, I'm not afraid to be fun and foolish. You've got to be able to laugh at yourself if you want to be fun. Besides, I love making people smile. I want to spread the *Loop of Love*! I want to dare to be different. I want to be the one face that sticks out in the sea of faces in a crowd.

When I do my daily "afternoon stroll" through our offices, I try to spread some energy and good cheer. Sometimes I'll make up and sing custom raps about my employees at company parties. Some people might think I'm a bit nuts, but it beats being boring!

Not many men in their forties, for instance, would relish going to a teen pop concert with thousands of screaming girls. But since I looked at the event as a fun "Daddy Day" with my daughter, I had a blast when we went to the Hannah Montana show! I took my daughter, Kelsey, and several of her friends to the concert. What an event! We were whisked away in a limo after a quick feast at Chinatown restaurant and headed straight to the show. We sat in amazing seats, and Kelsey and her friends were beaming the entire time. The kids were screaming with excitement as another teen act, Aly & AJ, opened the show. It was Kelsey's first real concert, and we had an incredible time together. Hannah Montana (aka Miley Cyrus) finally took the stage, and Kelsey was singing and dancing all night long. It sure is fun to plan Daddy Days like that with your kids!

But life's not all fun and games. There will be tests and trials at every turn. Don't let those frustrations throw you off track. Take traveling, which can be very stressful and very frustrating. I was in a taxi line at the airport recently, and I noticed a lot of stressed-out people getting more and more worked up waiting for a cab. Now, you can choose to make faces and stamp your foot and complain, or you can go with the flow. Stressing out doesn't do you or anybody else any good. Just take a deep breath, keep things in perspective, and regroup. Place yourself in a better frame of mind by engaging in a fond memory.

What about money, which seems to be everybody's biggest worry these days? No one likes paying more at the pump or shelling out more money than ever for groceries. But remember, you can't take it with you!

Try to develop an attitude of prosperity and abundance. I've traveled much of the world, and one of the things that continues to surprise me is that some of the poorest places on earth seem to have some of the happiest, most content people. Those people may not have much, but they just seem to have a simple appreciation for life. It's ironic when you think about it. The wealthiest nation on the planet still appears to be the most stressed-out! Lighten up, people!

What turns on your "fun button"? Think about what makes you laugh or smile, and then do more of it! For me, it's spending time with my family, seeing my kids happy, making deals at work, and continuing to build a great company with great people. Making a difference in the lives of others is great fun for me. And remember this can even be in the little things.

The other day, for example, some of my guys were in Switzerland for the Euro 2008 soccer tournament. I knew it was the end of their day and they had been working hard and running 100 miles per hour. They had just finished a long, stressful day. So I Skyped them from my computer and serenaded them with the first line of the alma mater of the University of Texas: "The eyes of Texas are upon you, all the live long day!" Everyone in the office probably heard me and thought I was nuts, but I wanted my guys to know that we were thinking about them—even though they were working halfway around the world.

You have to go out of your way to find the fun and make work feel like play. No matter what your job is, you can make a difference—you can have an impact. Think about those guys at the Pike Place Fish Market in Seattle. They may be fishmongers, but they've turned their jobs into an incredibly fun experience. They've made their workplace into a live show, all day, every day. They throw fish and whoop it up and have a blast with their visitors and customers. They've turned their job into an event. How much fun are they having? Well, that fish market has become an international tourist attraction and the basis for a bestselling book! If those guys can make selling fish fun, what can you do to make an impact and have fun with your business?

Is every day going to be a "funfest"? Of course not. You're bound to get down every now and then and have a bad day. You can't expect to have a positive mind-set *all* the time. Life can be a game of troubled times and hardships. Sparkling moments occur only every so often. But you've got to figure out how to get to those sparkling moments. And how to get more of them. The good news is that you do have the power to change your own frame of mind. You control your attitude, so make a conscious decision to set the proper tone.

Let me make one more distinction about fun. Some workaholics might think having fun means goofing off and being lazy. Nothing could be further from the truth! There's a big difference between finding fun in your life and slacking off. You can be hard-working and ambitious and unbelievably successful and still have fun. Just go back to Sir Richard Branson—he's an example of a hard-driving, no-nonsense entrepreneur who is clearly living it up.

So no more excuses! Put some fun into your life, and strive to make your work more like play. Send your employer or boss a cool motivational video, or give everyone you work with a hug. Be a difference maker. Feel free to share the following powerful, motivational business-appropriate videos with your coworkers. See if you can watch them without getting goosebumps!

http://www.youtube.com/watch?v=vr3x_RRJdd4 (Free Hugs)

http://www.youtube.com/watch?v=4oAB83Z1ydE (Richard Branson and the "crazy ones" Apple commercial)

http://www.youtube.com/watch?v=-vB59PkB0eQ (clip from *Facing the Giants*)

http://video.google.com/videoplay?docid=4292904215380323959 (The World's Strongest Dad)

http://www.youtube.com/watch?v=MslbhDZoniY (Nick Vujicic on being happy)

Remember, you can work hard and still have fun. You just have to love what you do! Life is much too short to be trapped in a job or a work situation you dislike. Break out! If you're not enjoying your work, plan your escape. Think about what it is you'd rather be doing and begin to take the steps to create the life you desire. How else are you going to make both work and life fun? Start by doing just one thing every day that will bring you closer to your ideal life.

SMILE

A simple smile can brighten anyone's day. It sounds almost too easy, but it's true. A smile will lift your mood and put a bounce in your step. And it will give a boost to those you smile at! Become a professional optimist and watch how your world suddenly becomes more fun.

"Smile," starring Olubunmi Ogunyankin (Olu) on Nic Askew's website soulbiographies.com, is a five-minute film that says it all. Olu is currently earning her PhD in chemical engineering (emphasis in biotechnology) at the University of California, Davis, and she has a fervent desire to help eradicate terminal diseases. She is also a classical concert pianist and a second-degree black belt and international champion in Kenpo karate. I met Olubunmi at a conference in April 2008. She had such a smile and sparkle about her that she lit up the room when she walked in. Olu's smile reveals her zest for life. Check out the clip at www.youtube.com/watch?v=10Kho174BN0.

Study after study suggests that optimism is a trait that can be learned with practice. It all starts with an infectious smile. I've admitted before that I've even hired a person on the basis of a simple smile. Something in that smile—that sparkle—was enough to convince me that this person was going to be a great addition to my team. One of my top sales guys smiles during every phone call. His clients can feel it when he speaks. This year, he'll sell over $5 million and make a ton of money because of his great attitude.

If a smile can land you a job, imagine what it can do for your day-to-day outlook! Smile at people and see if they smile back. It's almost an automatic reaction: give a smile and get a smile in return. A smile also tells your brain that everything is good. Did you know that it takes fewer muscles to smile than it does to frown? Smiling also signals your subconscious to be more happy and positive. Next time you're feeling down, force a smile and see how it boosts your mood.

Just thinking positive thoughts can lift your spirits by sending subconsious signals to the brain that life is good. It's not that you can completely eliminate negative thoughts, but you can choose not to focus on them. When you've got pessimistic thoughts in your head, try not to dwell on them. You can recognize and acknowledge those thoughts, but make a decision to switch to a more positive mode. Fortunately, positive thoughts are a lot stronger than negative ones, so your subconcious will gladly follow you to a better place!

The tricky part is learning to control any negative "self talk." All those little things you tell yourself shape your outlook. If you're the type of person who is always thinking, *Nothing ever goes right for me* or *I just can't win*, then guess what? That's the message that you are internalizing and turning into reality! So shift it! Change it! Try speaking to yourself with more positive language. Why not tell yourself, "Everything always goes my way!" or "I'm having fun today!" Your subconcious will follow your self talk. We know that it's not what happens to you that determines your mood, but *how you react* to what happens to you that counts. *Choose* to look at the bright side, and your life will be a lot more colorful!

MAKING FUN FOR OTHERS

Sometimes all it takes is a smile. Or a simple observation. Or a gesture, a shake of the head, or a shrug of the shoulders. As you learn to have fun yourself, you'll learn to help others have fun.

Making others have fun is key to our business. If someone buys a ticket from us and then doesn't have fun at the event, he or she will be less likely to buy a ticket from us in the future. It's our job to make sure that everyone has fun!

The Masters golf tournament is always a tricky event for us because the market fluctuates so much on any given day. Badges can run $1,000 each and a few hours later shoot up in price to $3,000 each. One year, we were short on tickets because one of our suppliers failed to deliver on time, and our customers were waiting anxiously. So we entertained the customers by serving fine wine and socializing with them while they waited for the badges to be delivered, which we made happen rather quickly. Just this past year when the economy was down, we were previously committed to badges at prices that were too high. Customers who purchased our badges at one price were upset when we started offering new, lower prices for the tickets. They were upset and thought we were price gouging. Our employees met the situation head-on, explaining that the market changes quickly and that we have to lock in seats every year. We gave one customer a discount for next year, and she was extremely happy.

NO FEAR, NO REGRETS

I've got a feature article from an interview I did with the *Austin Business Journal*, and the headline reads "Don't Be Afraid!" I have the article framed on the wall in my office as a constant reminder that you can't let fear get in your way. It's not that you're never going to be afraid—you just have to get past the fear and do that hard task anyway.

I get butterflies in my stomach just like everyone else does. None of us are truly fearless; we all have to face fears head-on and forge ahead, no matter what. Whatever it is, just dive right into the middle of it. You can try to ignore the situation or stick your head in the sand, but chances are, the problem is not going to go away on its own.

When you do the things you fear—when you feel the fear and do something anyway—it gives you hope and confidence. That's how you make it fun. You ride the scary new roller coaster at Six Flags. You jump out of an airplane. You swing on that rope out into the lake. You bet the farm on taking over another company. You live with no excuses and no regrets! Action is the only real cure for fear—and on top of that, it's fun!

As for living with no regrets, well, that's up to you. You can't live in the past, but you can decide how to put your past into perspective. Take your past regrets and turn them into lessons for the future. Use those past mistakes to motivate you in the present. Don't saddle yourself with all that baggage from your history. After all, you can't saw sawdust!

Earl Campbell didn't let his history keep him down. Earl grew up in hard poverty in Tyler, Texas. But he landed at the University of Texas and

10 WAYS TO MAKE LIFE MORE FUN!

Here are ten simple ideas for putting more fun in your life right now.

1. Get together with an old friend.
2. Do something completely spontaneous.
3. Leave work early this Friday and go for an ice cream.
4. Volunteer, do a good deed, or help someone out.
5. Take a spa day and pamper yourself.
6. Surprise your spouse or kids with an unexpected "today" present.
7. Try a new family activity that lets you laugh at yourself.
8. Eat dinner at a brand-new restaurant.
9. Arrange a day to do only your favorite things all day.
10. Buy tickets to see your favorite band or sports team.

By the way, to that last point, we can help! Just visit www.TicketCity.com or call 1-800-SOLD-OUT (765-3688).

became one of the greatest college football running backs of all time. He graduated in 1977 and was the number-one draft pick in 1978, going to the Houston Oilers. After his successful football career, Earl has made his home in Austin, Texas. He has been involved in many entrepreneurial endeavors and is still as popular as ever. Way to go, Earl!

Your past can be your friend or your enemy. It's all about your perspective and attitude. *You* get to decide how to use your history. You can be haunted by your past, or you can use it to launch yourself to new heights. You can live with regret and bitterness, or you can be transformed by your life lessons.

Perhaps some of us are luckier than others. But I believe we make our own luck. I think we create our own opportunities. Life is an adventure, so we've got to live big and find the fun. When in doubt, take the Dr. Seuss philosophy to heart: "Today was good. Today was fun. Tomorrow is another one."

Another fun recommendation is to host a "soundhacking" party. This is where you watch a movie with your family or friends, but you turn the sound off—and you provide the soundtrack! Or even better, unplug your television for a month! Try listening to the radio instead of watching TV, like our grandparents used to. Get a conversation going among your group by asking a question and letting everyone give a two-minute answer. Ask your kids or your coworkers: "What has been your best, most exciting moment of the week?" or "What was the high point of your vacation?" Visit www.MakeLifeMoreFun.com for even more ideas to add some fun and frivolity to your life!

TAKE THE FUN FITNESS CHALLENGE!

Has anyone ever accused you of being "no fun"? C'mon, admit it. At one time or another, you've been a fuddy-duddy. A party pooper. A sourpuss. Find out whether you're the life of the party or a wet blanket with our unscientific Fun Fitness Challenge!

For each question rate yourself on a scale of 1–10, with 10 being "best/most often/always," and 1 being "lame or never." No cheating! Good luck answering our fourteen questions!

1. **When is the last time you took a day off to "play"?**
   Never/Can't recall—1 2 3 4 5 6 7 8 9 10—Recently

2. **How often do you see your best friend?**
   Never/Hardly ever—1 2 3 4 5 6 7 8 9 10—Very often

3. **Do you like most of the people at your work/office?**
   No; Everyone is toxic!—1 2 3 4 5 6 7 8 9 10—Yes; They're great!

4. **When is the last time you did something completely spontaneous?**
   Never/Can't recall—1 2 3 4 5 6 7 8 9 10—Recently

5. On a day-to-day basis, how optimistic are you?
Not at all optimistic—1 2 3 4 5 6 7 8 9 10—Very optimistic

6. How often do you visit new restaurants, clubs, or attractions?
Never/Hardly ever—1 2 3 4 5 6 7 8 9 10—Very often

7. Do you use/take all of your vacation time?
No/Never—1 2 3 4 5 6 7 8 9 10—Yes/Always

8. Generally speaking, do you like where you live?
No; I hate it here!—1 2 3 4 5 6 7 8 9 10—Yes; I love it!

9. How often do you exercise or participate in sports such as golf, tennis, swimming, running, yoga, etc.?
Never/Hardly ever—1 2 3 4 5 6 7 8 9 10—Very often

10. Do you have a happy and harmonious family/personal life?
No—1 2 3 4 5 6 7 8 9 10—Yes!

11. How often do you volunteer or give time to community organizations?
Never/Hardly ever—1 2 3 4 5 6 7 8 9 10—Very often

12. Do you enjoy traveling and discovering new places and things?
No/Never—1 2 3 4 5 6 7 8 9 10—Yes/Always

13. Do you feel you have enough free time?
No/Never—1 2 3 4 5 6 7 8 9 10—Yes/Always

14. How often do you do the "*wild thing*"?
Never—1 2 3 4 5 6 7 8 9 10—Daily

How did you score?

100–140: Congrats! You are one fun cat!

71–99: You're fun most of the time, but there's still room for more.

41–70: You've got fun potential, but you really need to find more fun.

13–40: Sorry, you're not much fun. Reread this chapter and get to work (or play)!

AMAZING PROFILES: BERT AND JOHN JACOBS

Two guys I admire who really celebrate life are Bert and John Jacobs, the founders of "Life is good." They're the tee-shirt guys from Boston. These guys are great! They're fun; they're exuberant; they always seem to have smiles on their faces. Their company motto is "Do what you like; Like what you do." It's perfect. I met Bert and John at a party while they were in Austin shopping for furniture for their eighty-year-old dad.

We were hanging out with these guys, playing basketball, and they really made an impression on me. Even with all their success, they're overflowing with energy and optimism. They love to have fun and just do their thing. And it all started with a little drawing of Jake, their mascot—a character with a big, contagious grin who shares the simple truth that "Life is good." Here's their story as found on www.lifeisgood.com.

THE LIFE IS GOOD STORY

In 1989, Bert and John Jacobs designed their first tee shirt. They knew nothing about the business.

For five years, the brothers hawked tee shirts in the streets of Boston and traveled the East Coast, selling door-to-door in college dormitories.

They collected some good stories, but were not very prosperous. They lived on peanut butter and jelly, slept in their van, and showered when they could.

Chicks were not impressed.

By the fall of 1994, heading home from a long, less-than-fruitful road trip, Bert and John were desperately searching for answers to keep the dream alive. Little did they know, the only answer they needed was back in Boston, hanging up on their apartment wall.

Jake's contagious grin, simple as it was, seemed to express everything the Jacobs brothers believed in.

One fateful September day, they printed up forty-eight Jake shirts for a local street fair in Cambridge, Massachusetts. They laid the shirts out on their rickety card table. By noontime, all forty-eight of those tees were gone. A star was born.

Soon Jake was introduced to local retailers, and his simple message of optimism was embraced like nothing the brothers had ever seen. As demand for product soared, Jake's team grew, and the Little Brand That Could began to spread across America.

Today, the New England–based brand stays close to its roots, with an emphasis on simplicity, humor, and humility. Through Life is good Festivals, positive products, and a steady dose of ping-pong, Jake's crew does its best to keep the good vibes flowing.

RULE #6
HAVE A BIG HEART. MAKE A DIFFERENCE.

Try not to become a man of success, but rather to become a man of value.
—Albert Einstein

"YOU HAVE NO WAY TO GET THERE? You live where?" I asked, after spending ten minutes on the phone with a lovely elderly woman. *What good is a ticket to the Olympics if you can't get there?* I thought, and my head was already spinning. It was the opening day of the 1996 Summer Olympics in Atlanta. TicketCity had set up an office in Atlanta; we'd been planning for these Games for years. The Olympics is big business for us, but we really have to hustle on site. So much of the wheeling and dealing in our business is timed to the last minute.

Now, on top of everything else that was happening a few hours before the opening ceremonies of the '96 Games, I had this seventy-year-old woman requesting a ticket to the big event. She desperately wanted to buy a ticket, but she didn't have any transportation. Finally, I told her, "What the heck, if you buy a ticket from me, I'll take you myself." I rushed out and rented a black Lincoln Continental, and I drove eighty miles outside Atlanta to pick her up and take her to the opening ceremonies.

I found a parking space as close as I could, and I walked her to the stadium and sat with her during the event. It turned out to be an unforgettable experience. We watched the ceremony, and I could see the tears of joy sparkle in her eyes. It was extra effort, but I figured you can either talk about customer service, or you can live it. Put up or shut up. After all, I was just doing whatever it took to give one of our customers an unforgettable memory.

The moral of this story? If you and your company are going to be successful, you have to have heart. You have to be willing to go that extra mile—or eighty miles in the case of my limo service experience at the Olympics! You've got to be willing and ready to make a difference, to really connect with people. Be polite. Be nice. Be patient. Take care of your customers. If you're gonna talk the talk, you better walk the walk!

When people call TicketCity, I want their experience to be a pleasant one, right from the get-go. I expect my employees to be enthusiastic and positive on the phone. I want that smile to come right through the phone to grab the client. I want our caring attitude to emanate from our website. I want every customer to be delighted by the entire experience.

Enthusiasm is contagious, and that's the kind of positive vibe I expect my employees to spread. Share the love! Treat everyone with respect and courtesy. Give them the royal treatment. Once someone buys a ticket from us, I want that person to be a customer for life! I want him or her to become part of the TicketCity family. And the way we do that is by putting heart into everything we do.

After all, we're not just selling tickets, we're selling an experience! There's a lot of emotion wrapped up in our events, and that's why we say "a better experience lives here." In many cases, we're helping dreams come true or helping people savor a once-in-a-lifetime experience—whether it's the Olympics, the Super Bowl, or a U2 concert.

We're in the business of creating memories, moments, and experiences. Think about it: Will you ever forget that first baseball game you took your son or daughter to? Will you be creating new memories when you take your daughter to that sold-out Hannah Montana concert? What about that incredible trip to see your favorite team in the championship? Obviously, these experiences are going to stay with you forever, and we're thrilled to give a helping hand in honoring that moment. Think about the Olympics, for example. You may be traveling halfway around the world with your family to see the greatest athletes on the planet compete in events that occur only once every four years. You may be sitting in a seat in the stadium where half the world wants to be at that moment. You may be witnessing history! Think Michael Phelps winning eight gold medals or Usain Bolt winning the gold and breaking the 100-meter world record at the 2008 Summer Games. That's pretty powerful stuff!

So it doesn't matter what business you're in. To be successful, you've got to put your heart into whatever you do. It goes way beyond customer service; it's about putting passion into your work. It's about diving in and getting involved. It's getting into your customer's head and considering his or her specific needs and desires. It's making it personal. It's renting a car and driving to pick up a client and escorting her to the Olympic Games. It's stopping to help someone fix a flat tire like Dallas Cowboys quarter-back Tony Romo did recently. That's the "heart" part!

But it doesn't stop with business. Having a big heart—and what you might call a "heart-smart business"—is not just a 9:00 to 5:00 proposition. Here's another brief example: I was on my way back from Super Bowl XLII in Phoenix, and I was in line at the airline ticket counter. I noticed some commotion up at the front of the line. A pregnant woman was there with her two-year-old son, and the young mom was in tears because the airline wouldn't let the toddler travel free of charge as a lap child. Apparently, the mother couldn't afford another ticket, and she was understandably distraught.

I decided to go to the front of the line to see if there was anything I could do. The ticketing agent's hands were tied, and she insisted that a seat had to be purchased for the child. So I offered my frequent flyer miles to buy the little boy a seat. Problem solved! The mom was happy, the airline was happy, and I was happy I could help.

The way I see it, there are two ways I could have approached the situation at the airport that day: I could have moaned and groaned about the delay and inconvenience, complaining about the pregnant woman and her toddler making a scene. Or I could have chosen to be proactive and considerate, trying to find a solution. Obviously, the latter choice worked out better for all involved. Was the airline ticket fiasco any of my business? No, but I made it my business by jumping in and getting involved. I'll never see that woman again, but maybe she'll "pay it forward" one day and help someone else out. Everyone wins when you have a heart, when you do good when you can to make a difference.

I relate this story not to toot my own horn, but to demonstrate that anyone, anywhere, and at anytime can have a heart and make a difference in the lives of others. There will always be a need for random acts of kindness. In fact, these good deeds will eventually come back to you in ways you might never have imagined.

Here's the kicker on my good karma at the airport that day. When I arrived home, I watched the game and discovered that the Super Bowl "square" that I was a partner in had come up a winner. And it wasn't just some little prize. I'm talking twenty grand here! Granted, I split the prize with two other people, but winning $7,000 is not bad! Was my sudden windfall just coincidence, or was it a karmic reward for my good deed earlier that day? You tell me! One way or another, the good comes back to you. The more you give, the more you receive!

I realize that it's not necessarily easy to put heart into everything you do. It requires putting yourself out there and taking some risks. You might be rejected, or you might fail. You might even look foolish. But you have to give it a shot!

Putting your heart into your work is no different than what the world's greatest athletes do. Many of these superstars are not necessarily the biggest or strongest or fastest. They just make up for it with heart. With pure, raw grit and determination. With strength of mind over strength of body. With an unrelenting fortitude and resolve. As the great coach Vince Lombardi once said, The difference between a successful person and others is not a lack of strength, not a lack of knowledge, but rather a lack of will.

As I mentioned, I was in Phoenix for Super Bowl XLII. It was the undefeated, perfect-season New England Patriots facing the upstart, underdog New York Giants. On paper (and just about everywhere else), the Patriots were the better team. They were heavily favored to win. Thus far in the season they had been unstoppable. Yet somehow—shockingly—

SNAGGING SUPER BOWL TICKETS

Getting Super Bowl tickets is not a task for the faint of heart. Today, with face-value tickets costing as much as $1,000, they are very difficult to obtain. The NFL allots only 500 total seats for the general public. Unless you are friends with the team owner, a major sponsor who spends a ton of money advertising with the team, or a suite holder at the stadium, your chances of getting Super Bowl tickets at cost are pretty much nil.

That's where TicketCity comes in. Clients are able to purchase tickets several different ways. They can request tickets by team, and if their team does not make it to the Super Bowl, then they are only out a convenience charge. Clients can also purchase tickets by the event, which locks them in no matter which team makes it, and they pay a guaranteed price. Or they can wait to see which teams are in the game and pay the price at that time. There are also other resources, such as eBay, StubHub! and Craigslist. Just remember if a deal is too good to be true, it probably is.

the Giants pulled off the biggest Super Bowl upset since Joe Namath and the Jets beat the Colts in Super Bowl III. Peyton Manning's little brother had that secret something needed to win that day. He had heart. That's the only explanation I have. Eli Manning almost single-handedly won the game, and he was named the Super Bowl MVP. He showed tenacity and a will to win. He never gave up. That's how you put heart into your game.

CREATING A HEART-CENTERED BUSINESS

It's easy to draw analogies about heart when you're talking about the worldwide stage and drama of the Super Bowl. But how do you put heart into the cubicles and conference rooms of corporate America? How does the average executive or manager or "worker bee" put their heart into their work? First of all, you can't be an *average* executive or manager. Having a heart-centered business requires getting the most out of your employees. It means that you've got to instill a caring culture into the DNA of your company, from top to bottom. You need to make sure that each and every one of your people is going way above and beyond in an effort to super-serve your customers.

That's just one reason why outsourcing can be so tricky. You automatically give up a great measure of control when your customer service reps are half a world away. I'm not saying it's impossible to find exceptional service when you farm out to a third party. I'm just stating the obvious: that it's much easier to influence and ensure excellent service if your people are all under your roof.

But don't just take my word for it! See what my TicketCity team has to say about being a heart-centered company: I asked several of my employees how they put heart into their work, and what it means to them to build a business based on heart. The response was immediate and, well . . . *heart-warming!* In fact, rapid response is just one of the ways to show you care. Speed, responsiveness, and due diligence are a big part of heart marketing. After all, people like to know that they are being heard. People like to get answers to their questions. It's as simple as responding in a timely manner to an e-mail or a missed phone call. This shows you care.

It's also important to *be present* with the people you're dealing with. Give that person your undivided attention. In a world full of multitasking, it's too easy to get distracted and do two or three things at once. Stop multitasking! Be present with the person you're talking with. Can't you tell when you're talking to someone on the phone and they're distracted, obviously doing something else, too? You don't like having less-than-full attention, so why give others the same thing? Focus on the person on the other end of the phone and give them the gift of your full presence!

Here are some of the examples my team shared of how they put heart into working at TicketCity.

- **Find the connection**: "I always try to treat the customer I'm dealing with like a friend of a friend. I may not know that person, but there has to be something I have in common with them."

- **Go the extra mile**: "Even if a customer calls and knows exactly what ticket they want to buy, I'll take an extra minute to look over the inventory and make sure they're getting the best seats for their money and make alternate suggestions."

- **Put people before profits**: "In many situations, I will guide my customers to seats that are cheaper because I believe they will have a better experience or a classic view of the game or event."

- **Develop a relationship**: "I put my heart in the customers' experience by getting to know them. By finding out what they like, what their kids and spouses are into. Having a bit of a personal relationship helps to build trust, and keeps an ongoing rapport."

- **Be present and involved**: "I immerse myself in my interactions with customers by treating each person as if I were going to the event with them."

- **Make it personal**: "Talk to them like a human being, without using canned responses, like you would talk to a good friend."

And here are a few more examples, directly from TicketCity staff members:

- "One client bought a Final Four package from me. He needed to find a wheelchair rental for his sister while they were in San Antonio. I googled medical equipment rentals and e-mailed them a list of providers in the area that would help them. It only took a minute, and they really appreciated it."

- "Even going back seven years ago, to when I was in sales, and up to today, people have told me that they could buy seats at a cheaper price or that they have been offered more money for their seats from another broker. But they still choose to go with us. They work with us because of our approach, sincerity, and honesty."

And finally this, from our IT group, behind the scenes:

- "I don't deal with customers directly, so I'm going to take a different angle. I put in every effort to make sure the customers' personal information is guarded carefully and that their Web experience is a smooth and simple process. From the moment they land on our page until they checkout, we will make real-time ticketing needs that concern customer privacy a priority. Any IT features that allow our sales and purchasing departments to provide better client experiences are moved to the front of the line, and anyone on my team will gladly drop everything to fix a broken order or a bad invoice."

CUSTOMER SERVICE VERSUS CUSTOMER EXPERIENCE

Forget customer service. It's just not enough anymore. Customer service in the traditional sense is the absolute *minimum* you can do! It's the baseline—the starting point. If you want to build a better business, you've got to create a better customer *experience*. You've got to *engage* your customers. Really *listen* and respond to their needs. Taking care of your customers and clients is as much an attitude as it is a practice.

What's the difference between customer service and customer experience? Customer service is answering the phone on the first few rings. Customer experience is answering the phone with an enthusiastic greeting and a big smile!

Customer service is on-time delivery. Customer experience is giving away free tickets, or an unadvertised bonus gift, along with the delivery!

Customer service is sending a thank-you e-mail. Customer experience is sending a handwritten card or note with a personal message.

Customer service is a smooth e-commerce transaction. Customer experience is free shipping and one-click ordering. (Just visit Amazon.com to see what I mean!)

Customer service is Sears. Customer experience is Nordstrom.

You get the picture. There's a big difference between the two, and it takes time, effort, and energy to create customer experience.

What else can you do to enhance the customer experience? For one thing, don't think of your customers as some big, faceless mass of anonymity! They are individuals—real people! Each and every person your company has dealings with is going to be different. Each will have unique needs and specific issues. That's why listening closely is so crucial. A canned script or automated response won't cut it. Everyone must be treated like

TEN SIMPLE WAYS TO MAKE A DIFFERENCE

There are dozens of little things you can do every day, whether at work or at home, to make a difference. Here are a few simple ideas to get you started:

1. Whether you're a small business or a large corporation, commit to donating a small (or large!) percentage of your profits to your favorite charitable cause.
2. Buy a coffee for the person behind you in the drive-through line. This will make both of you feel great!
3. Volunteer to coach your kids' teams. There are never enough parents who get involved in children's sports.
4. Register and remember to vote—even in the less glamorous, local elections!
5. Give blood! (You can donate blood every 56 days!)
6. Get some trash bags and some gardening gloves; then throw your kids in the car and drive around your block or your neighborhood and clean up the trash at the side of the road. (Don't be surprised if the neighbors jump in and join you!)
7. Take a stand about an issue you care about and write a letter to the editor of your local paper.
8. Visit your child's school and read to the class or talk about your career. (Depending on your child's age, of course!)
9. Look up an old teacher you admired and send a letter telling him or her about the positive impact he or she made. I recently took my old college professor to a Longhorn football game!
10. Volunteer to work for a community event.

the individual that he or she is. Each client or customer wants to be heard and respected, so actively listen. Speak to your customers and not at them. Call them by name. Take your business personally!

While each customer should be treated individually, you should also expand your definition of *customer* to include coworkers, vendors, employees, or anyone you come into contact with during the course of business.

Common courtesy is a lost art that goes a long way in improving the customer experience. It's not that hard to be polite, is it?

Naturally, training your employees to be completely customer-centric from day one is vital. As I've said before, if you build exceptional customer experience into every fiber of your company's DNA, it's a lot easier to

THAT'S THE
TICKET!

SUPER BOWL TICKET PRICES
THROUGH THE YEARS

Back in 1969, if you attended Super Bowl III when Joe Namath and the Jets upset the Baltimore Colts, you would have paid just $12 for a ticket. Fast-forward to 2008, when a face-value ticket to see the New England Patriots and the New York Giants in Super Bowl XXXVI cost between $700 and $900 per seat!

Here's a quick look back at the pricing of Super Bowl tickets over the last twenty-five years. Just for fun, we've also included the average cost of a World Series ticket and a ticket to the movies.

1983—Super Bowl XVII, Rose Bowl, Pasadena, California
Washington Redskins defeat Miami Dolphins, 27–17
Super Bowl ticket: $40
World Series ticket: $15
Average movie ticket: $3.15
1987—Super Bowl XXI, Rose Bowl, Pasadena, California
New York Giants defeat Denver Broncos, 39–20
Super Bowl ticket: $75
World Series ticket: $20
Average movie ticket: $3.91
1990—Super Bowl XXIV, Louisiana Superdome, New Orleans, Louisiana
San Francisco 49ers defeat Denver Broncos, 55–10
Super Bowl ticket: $125
World Series ticket: $25
Average movie ticket: $4.23
1993—Super Bowl XXVII, Rose Bowl, Pasadena, California

Dallas Cowboys defeat Buffalo Bills, 52–17

Super Bowl ticket: $175

World Series ticket: $25

Average movie ticket: $4.14

1996—Super Bowl XXX, Sun Devil Stadium, Tempe, Arizona

Dallas Cowboys defeat Pittsburgh Steelers, 27–17

Super Bowl ticket: $200–$350

World Series ticket: $25

Average movie ticket: $4.42

1999—Super Bowl XXXIII, Pro Player Stadium, Miami, Florida

Denver Broncos defeat Atlanta Falcons, 34–19

Super Bowl ticket: $325

World Series ticket: $40

Average movie ticket: $5.08

2002—Super Bowl XXXVI, Louisiana Superdome, New Orleans, Louisiana

New England Patriots defeat St. Louis Rams, 20–17

Super Bowl ticket: $400

World Series ticket: $60

Average movie ticket: $5.81

2005—Super Bowl XXXIX, Alltel Stadium, Jacksonville, Florida

New England Patriots defeat Philadelphia Eagles, 24–21

Super Bowl ticket: $500–$600

World Series ticket: $65

Average movie ticket: $6.41

2007—Super Bowl XLI, Dolphin Stadium, Miami, Florida

Indianapolis Colts defeat Chicago Bears, 29–17

Super Bowl ticket: $600–$700

World Series ticket: $65

Average movie ticket: $6.82

Source: BusinessWeek.com

Movie ticket prices provided by the Motion Picture Association of America

2009—Super Bowl XLIII

Prices are projected to be $800–$1,000 per ticket!

develop good employees. That attitude of great service permeates Ticket City and everything we do.

Our customer service operation is high energy. I believe we give the same kind of service you get when you enter a Four Seasons hotel. At the Super Bowl when a client is picking up their tickets, we do the small things, which are so big. We open the door for our guests. We offer them water, soda, or a cocktail. We chitchat with them on where they are from and what they are doing while they are in town. We offer them ideas and suggestions on what they should do, where they should go, and where they should eat during their stay. We make a conscious effort to make a difference to add value to their dream weekend adventure. We get them on the list to attend the big parties, and then after the event, we personally contact them to make sure they had an amazing time and will remember their adventure forever.

AMAZING PROFILES: TOM MCEWEN

Tom McEwen is not your typical rock star, but make no mistake—the legendary sportswriter is definitely a rock star! For more than three decades, McEwen has been synonymous with sports in Tampa Bay, Florida. Generations of sports greats and power brokers have mixed and mingled with McEwen.

I had the privilege of going to the Super Bowl with Tom a few years back, and even amid all that excitement, he's a celebrity. Everybody knows and loves him. Naturally, when you're credited with putting Florida on the sports map and a key figure in bringing the Tampa Bay Buccaneers to town, you're going to be pretty darn popular!

Except for when Tom attended the University of Florida and served as a tank and platoon commander in the Pacific in WWII, this fourth-generation Floridian has lived his whole life in Tampa.

Tom spent more then thirty years as the sports editor for the *Tampa Tribune*, becoming one of the most powerful and influential sportswriters in the state. He was voted Sports Writer of the Year an amazing nineteen times! During his reign as sports editor for the *Tribune*, McEwen did far more than cover the local sports institutions; he helped build them! Tom was a major force in bringing an NFL franchise to town, as well as getting his friend George Steinbrenner to set up the

Yankees' $35-million spring-training facility in Tampa. Tom was also instrumental in bringing the NHL and pro soccer to the area. This "Titan of Tampa" even has a street named after him outside Raymond James Stadium, where he's also credited with helping to bring the Super Bowl four times.

Tom's home on the Bay is lined with framed photos of himself with a who's who of sports legends: Bear Bryant, Jesse Owens, Johnny Unitas, Don Shula, Joe Namath. He's the author of *Gators*, a history of Florida football, and he has served on the Pro Football Hall of Fame selection committee for thirty years.

In addition to his numerous sportswriting awards, Tom is the recipient of the Associated Press Sports Editors' Red Smith Award for lifetime achievement, often considered sportswriting's Pulitzer Prize. He also has a $50,000 football scholarship named after him at the University of Florida. And the Tampa Chamber of Commerce created and awards the annual Tom McEwen Leadership Trophy to worthy civic leaders. (He was the first recipient.)

McEwen has been called the last of a dying breed of legendary sportswriters. He's a journalist who became almost as well known as the sports figures he covered. He's a sports insider who makes no apologies for befriending the athletes he writes about. Through it all, he banged out six columns a week for his newspaper and built an enormous and loyal following. Long since retired from the Tampa Tribune, Tom still writes for his own website, www.heytommcewen.com

Tom was always an avid golfer and fisherman, and he makes a great point about the value of learning to golf from a business perspective. He has said, "There's no other way you can spend four hours with somebody and ask any question you want to as in golf."

Most important, Tom has created a foundation with George Steinbrenner called the Gold Shield Foundation—a charity that educates the children of fallen police and firefighters. Tom McEwen *definitely* has heart!

PERFORMANCE

RULE #7
NEVER STOP LEARNING.

There are only two options regarding commitment. You're either IN or you're OUT. There's no such thing as life in-between.
—Pat Riley, 7-time NBA championship coach

IT WAS THE FIRST FOOTBALL GAME of the 2008 season. Texas was winning, but it wasn't very pretty, and defensive coordinator Will Muschamp was ticked. I was in the front row right in front of him, so I saw exactly what happened. Will was pissed. He slammed his fist against the ground to get the attention of his defense, and then things got really crazy. He ripped off his headset, cutting himself below his ear, and started bleeding—a lot. The coach ignored the blood, but his players didn't. The defense played the rest of the game to perfection.

As you know by now, I'm a big believer in constant learning and self-improvement. I also like to live and learn and pass it on. I'm convinced that one of the keys to success is a willingness to coach and be coached. There are times when you need to be the coach, and there are times when you need to be the student. Lead, follow, or get out of the way!

Ongoing learning, self-improvement, and coaching are extremely important to me because the more I develop, the more I can share with my company, which will ultimately make TicketCity a better organization. Continued education and self-enhancement is a win-win situation. You get to share your new knowledge and pass it on to your team. The day you stop learning is the day you stop growing. And the day you stop growing is the day you stop living.

You can never know too much, and you should never think you know it all. The fun part is, you don't know what you don't know! You've got to live each day looking for the lessons in life. No matter where you are or what you're doing, ask yourself what you can learn from the situation. Where's the lesson? What's working? What can I do differently next time?

Benjamin Franklin said that the definition of *insanity* is doing the same thing over and over and expecting different results. If something's not working, change it! Persistence is one thing, but sometimes common sense is more important. Try something else. Be flexible. If you're flexible, you're "coachable." And as long as you're coachable and willing to learn, you can learn success.

Many life and business coaches suggest that their students or clients do this simple exercise: Take a piece of paper and draw a line right down the middle. On the left side at the top of the paper write "What is working." On the right side at the top write "What is not working." Then start on the left side of the page and describe everything in your life that is working. Include areas of your life that you feel are important, whether it's work, fun, relationships, health, or finance. Now do the same for the left "What is not working" column. Keep going until you feel you have described everything you can think of. Then review the page. You may be surprised to find what's working and what's not. Once you have a better sense of where you are, you can create a new vision for where you want to be. This is one form of self-coaching that can be very eye-opening!

There are many examples of coaches who have changed what they were doing and wound up winning.

- UTEP's Don Haskins was willing to take a chance in 1966 and recruited a team of black players. This risk allowed him to take his team to national prominence, and he won the championship. He also played a key role in the evolution of college basketball.

- Bill Walsh of the San Francisco 49ers developed the West Coast offense, which changed NFL football forever.
- Phil Jackson used the triangle offense that his assistant Tex Winters created in the early '80s to great effect, enabling the Chicago Bulls and Michael Jordan to win six NBA championships in the '90s. Jackson's Lakers later won three championships with the triangle offense.

Sometimes when you change what you are doing, you do not enjoy immediate success. Maybe you've made more than your share of mistakes. That's good! Mistakes are how we learn and grow. I remember I used to watch *Superman* when I was a young kid, about five years old. I thought it would be great if I could don a cape and fly, too. So I got a big beach towel, tied it around my neck, and went up to a second-story window. I opened the window and climbed up on the ledge. I jumped—and plummeted to the ground! It was a very valuable lesson about gravity. I learned the hard way that you can't fly. But guess what? I never jumped out a second-floor window again!

So I went a little too far that time. But I learned to look before you leap. You've still got to stretch—you've got to try new things or you'll never know how far your capabilities will carry you. You've got millions of years of evolution and survival instincts on your side, so it's okay to push the edges and test your limits. If you never try, you'll never know!

CONTINUE TO LEARN

How do I "walk the walk" when it comes to learning and personal development? I take classes, work with executive coaches, attend conferences, and read, read, read!

I'm a huge proponent of executive training and coaching, and I know it's made TicketCity a better, more substantial company. I started getting involved in leadership groups and conferences in the early '90s by taking courses like Verne Harnish's "Rockefeller Habits." I actively participate in peer groups, like the Entrepreneurs' Organization, and every year I attend a high-level CEO conference at MIT called the "Gathering of Titans." About sixty or seventy CEOs come together to network, brainstorm, tackle challenges, and hear top speakers. Not only do you learn a great deal at events like this, but you also get to know other leaders and like-minded individuals—plus, you get to learn about yourself.

I participated in a special year-long program with the Stagen Leadership Institute in which an elite group of eighteen top executives met four times a year to work together with coaches and peers. There were workshops, one-on-one coaching opportunities, teleclasses, e-learning, and a lot of accountability systems to keep you on track. The Institute was created by Rand Stagen, a management-consulting company that works with clients like Southwest Airlines, Neiman Marcus, Sprint, and Nokia. The program was enormously helpful to keep me moving forward—constantly learning, growing, and improving.

Of course, the other way I stay sharp and keep learning is by networking with my colleagues and fellow executives and leaders whom I admire. I make it a point to hang out with smart, progressive peers who definitely keep me on my toes. Sometimes it's a lunch; other times we'll play golf or tennis. Whatever the case, I create opportunities to stretch by spending time with other successful people. There's a management maxim I've learned that says that you're only as successful as the people you hang around with. That's why I hang around with amazing people!

I also hang out with peers to get a handle on things that may happen in the future. At lunch the other day I was talking to a dear friend who has sold many companies and has been an advisor to TicketCity. We both think that this recession may last five years or more. Meetings like this help me in my decision-making processes.

I also meet with peers to discuss new opportunities or learn about new systems that may enhance TicketCity's productivity. I was discussing Twitter and Facebook with a peer the other day. TicketCity already has a Facebook account that we actively market, but we decided to set up a Twitter account and spend more time with other social networking sites to continue to increase TicketCity's online presence.

COACHING OTHERS

In addition to my personal development, we do a tremendous amount of training and coaching within TicketCity. Previous experience is important, but training is even more essential to our growth and success. We empower our employees and set them up to succeed. Our coaching never ends; we have one-on-one meetings all the time. I have lunches with every employee, regardless of his or her role within the company. I send out company letters. I communicate constantly with the troops. As I've said before, we're also a very open and transparent company—so everyone knows what's going on and everyone is in a position to contribute.

In the early 1990s when TicketCity was just a baby, a business coach locked us in a room and helped us come up with a plan. We came up with our company mission statement, our core values, and our direction. He held us accountable for the direction we chose, and we were able to blossom and become one of Austin's fastest-growing companies.

I am constantly coaching employees. I have an hour meeting once a week with each member of my management team. They let me know what they are working on, and I hold them accountable to complete their tasks. We often come up with amazing ideas and opportunities in those weekly meetings. During one meeting, my VP of marketing came up with the idea to build our own in-house software system. That system has helped TicketCity grow to over $30 million in revenue per year without relying on an outside vendor to make sure our office is consistently running properly.

There are many other successful corporations that understand the value of training and coaching. You may have heard of the McDonald's Hamburger University or Disney University. Some companies are almost maniacal in their devotion to teaching and learning. Florida-based Physician Sales and Service (PSS), founded in 1983 by Pat Kelly, is one such company known for intensive training.

In addition to extensive, sixteen-week sales training, PSS has its own "university" for leadership development, where leaders can impart the company's culture and immerse employees in the right environment to make sure they've got what it takes to succeed. According to former CEO Pat Kelly's book, *Faster Company*, their basic training is rigorous and includes everything from personality testing to selling skills to nuts and bolts. At one time, PSS had eight different formal training programs, which included special courses such as "Experts Only" and "Profit College."

SET THE TONE

One of the keys to successful staff coaching is listening. It goes back to my L-A-E-R approach: Listen, Acknowledge, Explore, and Respond. If you're as good a listener as you are a coach, chances are you can help someone come up with an answer or solution on her own. You provide some perspective that helps her along, but she arrives at the answer herself.

How do you become a good listener? Well, you shut the hell up! Just resist the urge to jump in, and let the other person do the talking. This is a struggle for me because I can ramble with the best of them! But you've got to really listen—even if it means long, awkward pauses or uncomfortable silence. That's okay! Think before you speak.

As the leader, you've also got to coach by setting the example. Set the tone. If you expect your staff to have a good, solid work ethic, make sure they see that *you* have a strong work ethic! Can you teach work ethic? I think 80 percent of it can be taught and learned, and about 20 percent is hereditary: you are either born with the "hard work" gene or not. But I really think good work habits can be developed.

In order to be a great coach, you have to be passionate about making a difference. You see it with the great coaches in sports. They motivate and inspire their players. They maximize the potential of those athletes. The great coaches command respect, but at the same time they empower their players. The coach sets the tone.

Coach Mack Brown of the Texas Longhorns sets the right tone at the beginning of every football season. Each year he has a theme that his players wear on wristbands. In 2005, the team wore wristbands with the initials TDA, standing for "Take Dead Aim," and they won the national championship with Vince Young. Now there's a coach that knows how to set the right tone.

The coach must motivate—whether it's his players or his coworkers. How do you get passion out of your players? How do you get the most out of them? How do you get them to give their heart and soul to your cause?

First, they have to respect you. You've got to act in a way that commands respect. One of the ways I do that is by empowering my people and letting them know that I trust them. Trust is a two-way street. When you've developed trust and respect with your team, they will fight, scratch, and claw their way to victory for you!

TicketCity works by what I call an open-book philosophy. Everyone at TicketCity, from part-time employees to managers, knows everything about TicketCity. They know our daily sales numbers, our budgets, and our yearly expenses. Our employees are empowered to make decisions for the good of the whole, and I love when they are not afraid to take risks. As long as they can answer yes to the questions *Is this risk right for me? Is it right for my peers? Is it right for the company?* and *Is it right for the customer?*, they just do it. Every year at the Masters I watch the team work from dawn until 10:00 p.m. making sure clients and guests have the most amazing experience. Our empowerment philosophy enables us to fulfill our mission of "a better experience lives here."

Can you go too far to fire up your team? Maybe. Just ask former Mississippi State football coach Jackie Sherrill who, before playing the Texas Longhorns, once castrated a live bull in front of his entire football squad! He caught some flak for that one, but you can bet his team never forgot that—and they won their game!

Obviously, you want peak performance out of your team. Whether you're talking football, baseball, or business, that means planning, preparation, and practice. I recall preparing for the Beijing Olympics. For us, planning included creating contingency plans and running through all kinds of scenarios. We had a limited window to maximize our opportunities there, so we really had to be proactive. We planned and we reviewed our course of action, and then we fine-tuned everything because I really needed my guys to be top of things. The Olympic Games happen just once every four years, so we have to be prepared.

Sometimes we practice and prepare for situations that may never occur, but we have to be ready for anything. When I was in Hawaii recently, I was out on a boat, and I saw a lot of activity not far from us. I asked the captain what was going on, and he said the Navy Seals were practicing. They practice their maneuvers and drills over and over and over again so that it's second nature when the real deal happens.

The same is true for the Olympic athletes when they prepare for their events. Practice. Practice. Practice. As Vince Lombardi once said, "Practice does not make perfect. Only perfect practice makes perfect." It's like Larry Bird taking free throws for hours on end. Or the tennis players at Wimbledon who run three miles after completing their matches, just to stay in top condition. It's that extra effort that makes the difference.

I remember selling tickets to a special television boxing match a while back. The match was part of a reality TV show called *The Contender*, hosted by Sugar Ray Leonard and Sylvester Stallone. All these up-and-coming boxers competed on national TV each week, with the finals held in Las Vegas.

I met some of these guys, and they're all the same size, and they're all in incredible shape. All the contenders were pretty evenly matched; they all had about the same speed and skill. So what is it that separated the one champion from the other eleven boxers? What's that tiny little something that makes a winner? I believe it is heart that creates passion, perseverance, and mental toughness. That's why you've probably heard the phrase "the heart of a champion!"

Having this kind of grit and determination doesn't mean you have to be all macho and tough. If you're willing to learn and be coached, sometimes you've got to let your guard down. It's okay to show some vulnerability. You gotta open up. Talk to your coach or your boss. Keep an open mind and don't be afraid to ask for help! People appreciate vulnerability and sincerity. It's not all about testosterone and being a hard-ass. You're only human, so don't be afraid to show it.

During the 2007 World Series, when Alex Rodriguez and his agent, Scott Boras, were holding out on the Yankees for a new contract, Boras was playing the tough guy—the bad cop. The superagent was playing hardball, and it looked like a deal with the Yanks might not come together. The sides were far apart, but A-Rod really wanted to stay in New York. So, in an unusual move, Rodriguez went around his agent and reached out directly to the team's front office. Maybe Rodriguez showed a little humility and vulnerability. Well, that move paid off big-time! A-Rod ended up with a record-setting ten-year $275 million dollar contract with the New York Yankees. He now makes more money per year than the entire Florida Marlins baseball team combined!

Realize—and accept—that you don't know it all; you're not necessarily the smartest guy or gal in the room. Remember that you don't know what you don't know! Be open and flexible and willing to learn.

YOU CAN'T COACH LUCK, OR CAN YOU?

We've all had our experiences with luck, both good and bad. Luck has played a part in my business as well as everyone else's. Although we've all experienced luck, it's something that we can't teach or learn. What exactly is it? According to the dictionary, *luck* is defined as "a chance happening, or that which happens beyond a person's control." Luck can be good or bad, as in good fortune or misfortune.

Luck has been a popular topic for coaches through the ages. How many of these quotes have you heard before?

"I'm a great believer in luck and I find the harder I work, the more I have of it."

—*Thomas Jefferson*

"Shallow men believe in luck. Strong men believe in cause and effect."

—*Ralph Waldo Emerson*

"Everything in life is luck."

—*Donald Trump*

"Luck is when opportunity knocks and you answer."

—*Author Unknown*

"Luck is what happens when preparation meets opportunity."

—*Seneca*

Any way you look at it, luck is something we all covet. Who doesn't want Lady Luck to smile upon us? Good fortune is indeed a good thing. But what is *luck*, really? Do we actually create our own luck, or does fate play a role in our success?

TICKETCITY'S TICKET-BUYING TIPS

March Madness

Sixty-five college basketball teams compete for the top spot in the NCAA Tournament known as March Madness. Meanwhile, thousands of eager fans also compete to find the best tickets available. Unlike college football bowl game announcements, which allow fans time to arrange travel plans while buying tickets, college basketball fans have only four days to find tickets before the tournament begins. With more than eighteen years of experience in the ticketing industry, TicketCity offers a few tips for buying March Madness tickets:

- Check with the ticket source. The venue box office where your team will play should be your first stop. Next, check with your school to see how it is allocating tickets for alumni. NCAA Tournament tickets typically sell out early at the venue box office. Schools usually have just enough tickets for staff, family, and big alumni who donate to the athletic department.

- Always check the secondary market. Once you know what options are available through the venue and your school, compare those to prices on the secondary ticket market. Depending on the demand for your team's region, you can often find better seating locations and even lower prices on the secondary market than at the box office.

- Buy tickets ASAP. With only a few days between when the brackets are announced and the tournament games begin, inventory and prices in the secondary market fluctuate continuously. The demand for NCAA Tournament tickets traditionally increases as teams advance. One suggestion is to consider buying tickets for the Regional Finals and/or Final Four early. If your team fails to move beyond the early rounds, reselling tickets is always an option. Most ticketing companies such as TicketCity will buy and sell tickets to the tournament.

- Enjoy the game. Once you've secured your tickets, enjoy one of the most exciting sporting events in the world. The passion of thousands of screaming fans at a March Madness game is an experience that every sports fan should have at least once in her life.

You can certainly debate whether good luck is a matter of fate or whether it's something you create. My own belief is that we create the *opportunities* for luck to flourish and that this is something we can coach others to do. Things have a much better chance of falling into place if we create the right circumstances. Control the things you can control, and take calculated risks on the rest!

I find that when I take chances, I get lucky. So don't be afraid to put yourself out there. You've got to be in the game if you expect to win! Sure, fate may play a role, but only if you're prepared for it. In other words, if you want to be at the right place at the right time, you need to put yourself at the place!

If you want to be lucky, you also have to have the right attitude. Keeping yourself open to lucky breaks and possibilities means maintaining a "lucky" attitude. It starts with you internally; it's an "inside" game that doesn't necessarily depend on external circumstances. Act lucky and get lucky. Expect the best and you'll often get it!

Sorry, luck has nothing to do with lottery tickets! It's fine to have "a dollar and a dream," but that's probably not going to make you a lottery winner. Even when opportunity knocks, you still have to get up and open the door!

Some folks might call it luck that TicketCity did so well with the Sugar Bowl in 2008. No one could have predicted for sure that LSU would play there and that the football game would become such a hot ticket. Still, we took some early risks. We purchased a lot of tickets for the Sugar Bowl. We took a chance and went out on a limb, and it paid off in spades. The Sugar Bowl was huge that year, and we scored because we created the opportunity to be "lucky." I'll take that kind of luck anytime!

Create the potential for good things to happen. Put yourself in the midst of circumstances that will create so-called lucky breaks. Take chances and risks. You may be pleasantly surprised how your luck can change, and how you can coach others to improve their luck!

In some cases, you may have to be the coach, and in others you've got to be willing to be coached. Know when it's time to lead, and when it's time to listen. As a leader and a learner, your role is going to change depending on the situation. It's up to you to figure out when it's appropriate to teach and when it's time to be taught. Know when to step up and coach and when to be humble and learn.

AMAZING PROFILES: RICHARD GARRIOTT

Richard Garriott is a man who personifies passion. His enthusiasm and his heart have driven him to a life of excitement and adventure. After all, it's not every civilian that can lay claim to the title of space traveler. In fact, Garriott became the sixth "space tourist" when he ponied up $30 million to fly to the International Space Station in October 2008.

As it turns out, the British-born but Texas-raised Garriott was following in his father's space boots, as his scientist father, Owen Garriott, was an astronaut who flew with Skylab 3 and on the space shuttle. When the younger Garriott traveled to the Space Station, he became the first offspring of an American astronaut to go into space. "This mission to the ISS fulfilled a lifelong dream to experience spaceflight as my father first did thirty-five years ago; it's an honor to be the first American to follow a parent into space," Garriott told reporters at the time.

Richard Garriott was born in Cambridge, England, but was raised in Nassau Bay, Texas from the time he was a baby. While at Clear Creek High School, he took an interest in computers and programming. When Garriott was sixteen, his parents sent him to a computer camp, where he continued to explore his love of computer programming. By the time Garriott entered the University of Texas at Austin, he had already produced his first successful computer game, Akalabeth.

By the early '80s, Garriott had developed the Ultima computer game series, which became so popular that he established Origin Systems, his own video game publisher. Origin went on to become one of the most influential game developers in the history of video games. Garriott eventually sold Origin to Electronic Arts in 1992.

In October 2008, Garriott made his journey into space on the *Soyuz* along with two cosmonauts. He spent eleven days in space on board the International Space Station, where he took part in several educational outreach programs.

Garriott's passions go beyond the realm of computer gaming and space travel. His diverse adventures have included acting as a "corner man" for friend and professional boxer Jesús Chávez, and he is an avid and accomplished magician. Garriott even built an impressive haunted house and magic museum at his Austin residence, Britannia Manor.

As for Garriott's plans after returning from space, he told *Time* magazine, "I am a devout explorer of the reality in which we live, so this is by no means my first exploration—but it's a big one. It's the biggest. But I still have on my list visiting disappearing indigenous populations around the globe, which I have yet to do, and Southeast Asia is still an area to me which is largely unexplored, and I still have a lot of things in the deep oceans that I hope to do. Plus, you know, I hope this isn't my only spaceflight."

Garriott's passion, curiosity, and love for exploration—and learning—will no doubt ensure that his adventures continue.

RULE #8
TAKE CHANCES. PUT YOURSELF OUT THERE.

Only those who will risk going too far can possibly find out how far one can go.
—*T. S. Eliot*

BEING IN THE TICKET BROKERAGE BUSINESS, one of our biggest and most important events in recent times was the 2008 Summer Olympics in Beijing. As big and spectacular as this global event is for the world, it's just as big for my company. You could even say that our future depended on it.

For TicketCity, the 2008 Olympics meant months of planning and preparation. Diving headlong into the Summer Games in Beijing was a huge risk. Talk about betting the farm! As a ticket company, navigating the 2008 Summer Olympics was like swimming through shark-infested waters with storms raging all around and no land in sight!

Here we were halfway around the world in a Communist country—a very closed society. We were dealing with a different language, an unfamiliar culture, and a strict government—all the while trying to do business and, hopefully, making a profit. On top of that, we were buying and selling in three or more different currencies—U.S. dollars, Chinese renminbi (RMBs), and euros.

Normally, TicketCity handles big events such as the Super Bowl, the Masters, and the Kentucky Derby. We acquire and sell our seats, and thus enable dreams to come true. However, for the Olympics, we had 302 events in twenty-eight categorie crammed into less than three weeks! Picture three hundred Super Bowls over sixteen days, with many occurring on the same day! It's madness. Insanity. Chaos. But for us, it was business (not quite) as usual.

We had so many factors working against us, but we did what we had to do to succeed. And success for us is not just making a buck—it's making memories for our customers. It's making sure that we provide them with that once-in-a-lifetime experience. It's helping their dreams come true!

Now, that's not always an easy thing to do, even under the best of circumstances. In Beijing, we had to do that while wading through thousands of tickets, hundreds of clients, and dozens of unique challenges. We rented an office space on the nineteenth floor of a building in Beijing and hired some local staff. The Chinese staff members were phenomenal. They learned our software and systems in one day and began selling up a storm!

But the logistics involved in Beijing were crazy. We were taking care of our clients, fulfilling last-minute customer requests, and buying and selling thousands of tickets. In the meantime, anyone caught selling even one Olympic ticket on the street was immediately thrown in jail for ten days! See ya, wouldn't want to be ya!

As difficult as it was for me to keep a low profile, we really tried to stay on the down-low in Beijing. We posted ads selling tickets on the local classified Internet site called TheBeijinger.com, which is similar to craigslist. We focused on filling our orders and working with other American and European companies that were set up in Beijing buying and selling tickets. Our office was in a prestigious central location in downtown Beijing, and word got out pretty quick that we were the go-to guys to help people get seats to those hard-to-get sold-out events. I'm sure the Chinese government knew we were there, but as long as we didn't flaunt that we were selling tickets, they left us to ourselves. The Chinese are all about respect.

If you disrespect their laws by selling tickets on the street, then they'll take action and make an example out of you. We made sure our employees took extra tickets out to the street as rarely as possible.

Along with the threat of jail time looming over our heads, the government wouldn't let us send out tickets by Federal Express. They didn't want tickets being sent in or out of the country, so we had to figure out other ways to get our clients their tickets to the Games. We ended up having the clients meet us at our downtown Beijing office to pick up their tickets. The customers were frustrated at first, but then they realized we were able to help them with valuable information because we were so familiar with Beijing. We pointed them toward great restaurants, shopping areas, and sightseeing opportunities. The face time with the clients was priceless.

We also had the challenges of our prepaid ticket sources not delivering us our tickets, couriers losing tickets, and last-minute cancellations from our suppliers. All the while, we were dealing with a thirteen-hour time difference with our home office in Texas.

We even had an undercover newspaper reporter buy tickets from us and then write a big exposé. That story put our entire operation at risk. At one point we were so concerned about the article we literally closed down our operation and regrouped at our Beijing apartment to figure out what to do. We had so many people that still needed to pick up the tickets that they had ordered back in the U.S. that we forged ahead and stayed the course in our downtown office. This was just another firestorm, but we were able to work through it.

In some respects, you could say we had as much at stake at the Olympic Games as the athletes themselves. Our careers were on the line. We were under incredible pressure. We had practiced long and hard for this spectacular event. We were shorthanded, overburdened, and under intense pressure. My team worked from 8:00 a.m. to 2:00 a.m. most days, with no real downtime. I couldn't be any prouder of my team for stepping up and going above and beyond expectations. They really created their own gold medal performance while at the games.

At one point, after we had been going nonstop for days, I finally kicked everyone out of our office at 9:00 p.m. and took the gang to dinner. We needed to decompress and catch our breaths. As the leader, I had to keep my team motivated, healthy, and productive. I had to know when it was time to stop everything and give my team a critical break. We all went for an amazing dinner at Lan, one of the most famous restaurants in Beijing. I wanted to give my team the limo treatment because they had been working their tails off.

The dinner at Lan was amazing! Located high up on the top floor of a famous mall in downtown Beijing, the restaurant had a bright, prestigious art-deco vibe with furniture that made you feel like you were on another planet. The manager put us in a private hand-painted room, and we sat down at a round table built for fifteen people. The tabletop turned so it was easy for everyone to share the food and wine. The dinner was extravagant, and my team loved it.

Back at the office, we hired locals and translators to help us out on site, and they were outstanding. They learned quickly and were a tremendous help. That's why I believe in empowering your people. Hire good people and get out of their way. There's a great quote from Theodore Roosevelt that illustrates the point perfectly: "The best executive is the one who has enough sense to pick good people to do what he wants done, and self-restraint enough to keep from meddling with them while they do it."

Just like the athletes, my team was prepared, dedicated, experienced, hardworking, and showed grace under pressure. These attributes are all the makings of a champion—whether you're swimming for gold medals or just meeting the commitments you've made to your customers.

After all, many of our clients traveled halfway around the world and spent thousands of dollars to be in Beijing. Our job was to make damn sure they were taken care of. Opening ceremony tickets were selling for as much as $15,000 apiece! That seems nuts, but it was simply a matter of supply and demand.

One of our clients ordered over 4,000 event tickets, valued at millions of dollars. We believe the tickets were for a guerilla-marketing ploy by Nike. The order was taken from our Austin office, and the tickets had to be delivered on an event-by-event basis in Beijing. So we prepared the best we could, but in the end, we just had to figure a few things out on the fly. We had to think on our feet and come up with workarounds for any obstacles that got in our way.

And with more than three hundred events, we had to gauge what was going to be hot, and what was not. There's a lot of risk-taking and guesswork involved in reviewing events like gymnastics, track and field, badminton, swimming, diving, basketball, and tennis—and choosing Category A, Category B, and Category C tickets. Helping our clients get the best tickets so they can have the best possible experience was a priority.

Every event was a big ticket in Beijing, but the hottest events after the opening ceremonies were the swimming events with Michael Phelps and the diving events with the Chinese divers. Gymnastics and basketball with Yao Ming were also huge, as well as badminton, which is a national pastime in China.

The most anticipated event in track and field was the men's 110-meter hurdles. Liu Xiang, the 2004 Olympic champion and one of the most popular Chinese Olympic athletes, was favored to win. He was a Chinese superstar, and all eyes were looking forward to watching him win a gold medal for China. Then he withdrew from the race with an injured Achilles tendon in his right foot. As soon as he withdrew from the event, the prices of tickets plummeted.

But TicketCity did whatever we had to do to make the Games a success. Before the Games started, I went around to all the hotel concierges to introduce myself. I let them know that we could get tickets for their guests. We worked with many of the sponsors, just building relationships and making introductions. In Chinese culture, formal introductions are very important.

My team showed a lot of character, and a lot of heart—again, not that different from the Olympic athletes themselves. During the opening ceremonies, for instance, one U.S. athlete is chosen by the others to carry the American flag. As you can imagine, that individual must be pretty special—he or she must have a lot of heart, compassion, and humility. It's a huge honor to be selected to carry the flag.

Keep in mind that there were 11,000 athletes from 204 countries participating in the 2008 Summer Games. The motto for the 2008 Olympics was "One World, One Dream." I think that's a bit ironic coming from a closed, socialist society like China, but they really nailed it. One of the things I love about the Olympics is what I call the "loop of love." This refers to the sharing and camaraderie that goes along with the Games. People from dozens of countries and cultures are intermingling, working and living together, and enjoying a common experience. Usually there's lots of trading and bartering going on, with people from different countries trading pins or Olympic souvenirs. There wasn't nearly as much of that in Beijing because the government was so strict. In fact, the government controlled the majority of the tickets, so that made things even more challenging. Still, we made sure that our customers were part of the big TicketCity "loop of love," and our clients really appreciated it.

The entire Olympic experience was an exercise in risk and reward for us. It was taking chances. Going out on a limb for our clients. Trying to minimize the downside. Dealing with enormous amounts of tickets while keeping a low profile in a Communist country. The largest Chinese bill is 100 RMB, and it's only worth about 15 U.S. dollars. So, you can imagine what kind of cash was changing hands when we were selling events that were $2,000 or more per ticket! We had to know the exchange rates and work in different currencies. It was all pretty intense.

As for our experience, it was phenomenal. My team stepped up to the plate and hit it out of the park. The 2008 Summer Olympics were a huge success for TicketCity. We had to think on our feet, improvise, react quickly, and stay in sync. We had to take chances and overcome obstacles. We worked as a team and got it done. We made amazing connections, and we were profitable, as well.

Beijing is an incredible city—even more crowded than New York City. The subway trains were packed like cattle cars. I could look down from my apartment and see thousands of people on the streets. The traffic was crazy, even though the Chinese government allowed vehicles on the road only every other day, depending on a car's even or odd license plate number. The city of Beijing set up barricades and special lanes for accredited vehicles. That presented a great opportunity for us because we were selling accredited vehicle passes. We also hired out translators. Wherever there was a chance to make a buck in Beijing, we'd just seize the moment! You've gotta love capitalism!

Despite all the challenges, we still had to take care of our clients and provide excellent customer service. A lot of our clients are high rollers and expect the best. For the most part we just sold tickets, but if there were special requests, we could provide tickets, accommodations, or anything else the guest wanted. We made some mistakes along the way, but we did our best to correct them quickly. When we goofed, we met the problems head-on and fixed them.

There were times we sent clients tickets from our Austin office to their home addresses, but they were already en route to Beijing. When the clients arrived and we didn't have their tickets, we had to take the hit and find them other seats. We lost a lot of money on these mix-ups, but it's not all about making money; it's about doing the right thing and making sure your customers who have traveled halfway around the world have an amazing experience.

As for my personal experience, I probably lost fifteen pounds in a couple of weeks in Beijing. I knew I had to stay healthy and energized, so I got up every morning at 6:00 a.m. to run and go swimming. Working fifteen to eighteen hours a day and eating meals on the fly, I knew I had to stay on a regimen that was healthy. You can't provide leadership if you're not mentally and physically prepared! I needed to be in top form to provide my team the coaching, the communication, the pep talks, the motivation, and the incentives for them to accomplish the nearly impossible.

While I didn't get to attend as many events as I would have liked, I did get to see Roger Federer win the gold medal in the men's doubles. You could see how much Federer wanted that win. It was extremely important to him. It really reminded me of my guys working in the trenches during the Olympics. Not unlike Federer, my team was digging deep and somehow finding that extra will to make sure they were taking care of our clients. That special something puts you over the top. Sure, there's a big difference between tennis and tickets, but if you want to do your best and win, that requires passion, energy, and heart!

When the Games were finally over, I took my crew out for another big celebration. We rented out a place called Tim's Texas BBQ in downtown Beijing, and we had a Texas-size feast. In the midst of our party, who shows up but Yao Ming and a few others from the Houston Rockets! So we even got to party and hang out with one of the biggest celebrities in all of China!

NO FEAR

The Olympics was another great example of my "don't be afraid" philosophy in action. We didn't have all the answers, and we didn't know exactly how it was going to play out. But we made a conscious decision to forge ahead into the unknown, without fear or apprehension.

For me, this philosophy goes all the way back to when I was a kid. We didn't have computer games yet, so I played Risk and Monopoly, where you had to roll the dice, take chances, and play to win. I loved a challenge and I hated to lose.

Years later, in August 2000, when we decided to buy a company called SoldOut.com (1-800-SOLD-OUT), we used the same fearless mentality. We took a big risk, but we rolled the dice and came out on top! We spent a quarter of a million dollars on a company that was in bankruptcy, and we used all of our cash, but we got lucky. SoldOut.com had a strong presence in New York, and that year, the Mets played the Yankees in the "subway" World Series. A few months later, the New York Giants played in the Super Bowl. We also did well with the U.S. Open in Flushing Meadows. Fortunately for us, the phone was ringing off the hook.

That purchase was a gamble that paid off. I'm not suggesting that we dove in carelessly without evaluating all the risks. We carefully weighed the decision to make the purchase, and we made strategic plans to avoid failure. I respect the opinions of my team, but the final call was mine, and sometimes you just gotta know when to take the plunge. You always need to be thinking two steps ahead and be willing to adjust your game plan on the fly. Be prepared, but be willing to make mistakes. Plan to win, but don't be afraid to fail.

PUT YOURSELF OUT THERE

Take risks. Be bold. Try new things. Don't be afraid to make a fool of yourself from time to time—especially in pursuit of a worthy goal.

We have an annual holiday party at TicketCity where we celebrate the wonderful year that our company had. We have a huge buffet dinner, do the white elephant giveaway that everyone loves, and give away prizes like round-trip tickets on Southwest Airlines, digital cameras, and plasma screen TVs. But that is not what everyone looks forward to. Every year I get all of our employees and their spouses to make a big circle around me, and I do a "Randy Rap." I ask everyone to help with the backbeat, and I rap short anecdotes about each person at TicketCity and that year's major events. I do this totally winging it, but it is still sincere and from the heart. Everyone enjoys the moment and laughs hysterically during the five-minute rap session.

I am not a rapper, but I take the chance, and everyone appreciates it. Don't be afraid to fail, because no matter what, you *will* make mistakes and you *will* fall down. The trick is getting back up again. One of my favorite quotes simply states: "Success is falling down nine times and getting back up ten."

Before we close this chapter on taking chances and going for the gold, let me share a great quote I came across that sums it up nicely. John Naber, four-time Olympic gold medalist said, "Although they only give gold medals in the field of athletics, I encourage everyone to look into themselves and find their own personal dream, whatever that may be—sports, medicine, whatever. The same principles apply."

AMAZING PROFILES: BODE MILLER

I had the unique pleasure of meeting alpine skier Bode Miller at the 2006 Winter Olympics in Torino, Italy. It was during these Olympics that Bode was widely criticized for his alleged "party boy" antics. In fact, *Newsweek* magazine cited his "frat boy larks" and named him "America's Top Ski Bum." The controversy has since died down, but Bode has continued to amaze the sports world, win World Cup titles, silence critics, and—most of all—go his own way.

Bode is my kind of athlete: confident, unconventional, and fiercely independent. Does he like to have fun? Sure. Does he follow his own path? No question. But is he still one of the best skiers on the planet? Absolutely!

Anytime you go against the grain and break the so-called rules, you're going to attract some attention. And Bode has had his share of the spotlight—both good and bad. But his incredible talent and love for the sport are undeniable. Above all, Bode Miller is a winner.

Those who got a glimpse of Bode the "playboy" in Torino missed the point. That was pure Bode, bucking the system, refusing to kowtow to the media or the Olympic machine, and marching to the beat of his own drum.

Even just sharing a few beers with him during the Olympics, I found him to be thoughtful, engaging, articulate, and authentic. He's the real deal. Having grown up in northern New Hampshire, quite literally in the woods and in a home with no electricity, Bode learned self-reliance and character at an early age. When he wasn't on skis, says his mom, he was barefoot, hiking through the woods and communing with nature.

Bode's hometown, Franconia, New Hampshire, in the state's "North Country," is known for producing individuals with small-town values and big opinions. Bode grew up in a community of strong, self-sufficient, and independent people who personify New Hampshire's motto of "Live Free or Die." Bode may be a bit gruff and unrefined, but he's got that distinctive, independent streak that makes him one of the greatest skiers in the world.

On and off the slopes, Bode breaks with convention, uses his instincts and his intellect, and isn't afraid to blaze his own trail. "I just don't respond well to orders," Bode admits in his autobiography, *Go Fast, Be Good, Have Fun* (Villard, 2005). "And I follow advice only if I ask for it—and I never ask for it," he says. He's a loner and a free thinker. "He never listens to anybody," says his coach and uncle, Mike Kenney, in a recent magazine interview. "He's always fully confident in his decisions. He keeps breaking rules." And, he keeps winning.

The silver medalist has been clocked at 100 miles per hour, making Bode one of the fastest skiers in the history of the sport. He won the World Cup overall title in 2005 and again in 2008. His coaches and trainers say that there are many reasons for his success, but they observe that Bode is calm, confident, and focused in high-pressure situations. In addition, he's tough on himself and holds himself to incredibly high standards. Agility, balance, and lightning reflexes don't hurt, either!

I admire Bode because he's a phenomenal athlete, but I also admire his attitude and philosophy. You've heard me talk about the "book of good," and it sounds like Bode is reading from the same playbook. Here's one of the things he had to say in his autobiography: "I always err on the side of good; things never go badly with good—that is, simple niceness, a smile, a nod, a gracious reply. Niceness will always pay off . . . One good deed begets another—I see it too often to doubt it. Call it viral niceness."

However, my favorite passage from Bode's book has to be this one, and I agree 100 percent: "I'm a citizen of the United States of America, and to me that means that life's purpose is the pursuit of happiness—'pursuit' being the operative word. Happiness isn't an excuse to slack; it's an opportunity to be your best, to create a life's work, to make your mark. If this is news to you, then it's definitely time to get off your ass and do something extraordinary. Happiness awaits."

Go Fast, Be Good, Have Fun. That expression is both the subtitle of Bode Miller's book and the words he lives by. He's my kind of guy!

RULE #9
BE A ROCK STAR! WORK HARD AND PLAY HARD.

As a rock star, I have two instincts: I want to have fun, and I want to change the world. I have a chance to do both.
—U2's Bono

WHEN PEOPLE HEAR THAT I've been in the ticket business since 1990 and have attended events at hundreds of musical venues, they often wonder what my most memorable concert experience is. You may be surprised by the answer! The Rolling Stones? Nope. Bruce Springsteen? No. Boston from back in the day? Awesome, but still not my all-time fave. How about U2, Garth Brooks, Billy Joel, Elton John, Aerosmith, or the Grateful Dead? No, guess again! It's not even one of the times I was able to go backstage and meet the musicians or when I had amazing seats in the front row.

My most memorable concert experience ever has less to do with the music and more to do with the memory. My all-time favorite show was taking my fourteen-year-old twin boys and a couple of their friends to see Van Halen. (I must admit that I love hard rock: my boys' names are AC and DC—Alec Cohen and Derek Cohen!) We had an amazing time.

We jumped in the truck and road-tripped to Dallas on a Saturday afternoon. It was lead guitarist Eddie Van Halen's birthday, so we knew the concert was gonna be awesome! Eddie's teenage son, Wolfgang, is now the bass player for the band, and he played by his dad's side the entire night. Eddie was so proud of his kid that you could see him beaming. Van Halen played for nearly two and a half hours, and my kids did not sit down once! It was their first really big rock-and-roll concert, so we did it up right. The kids were jumping up and down for most of the songs, and when "Jump" came on, they almost launched out of their shoes! It was a great rock-and-roll Dad Day with my boys—one of those rare, cross-generational bonding experiences. It was awesome to see them enjoying good old-fashioned rock-and-roll, just like their old man! We had a blast!

I WANNA BE A ROCK STAR!

In the flurry of e-mails you receive on a daily basis, what are your favorites? What are the ones that make you feel good? What are the notes that stand out? For me, there's no greater compliment than a brief "You rock!" expressed in an e-mail or, better yet, said on the phone.

For some reason, being told that we "rock," or that we're "rock stars," makes us feel tremendous. When I'm sending notes or getting instant feedback on a social networking site like Facebook, I love it when friends or colleagues post a quick "You're such a rock star!" to me. It's the ultimate compliment and a great way to say thank you.

And why shouldn't we feel great when we're told we rock? Who wouldn't want to be a rock star in their industry? Being a rock star implies that you're popular and admired, to say nothing of the cool factor. If you're the Bono or Madonna of your particular field, isn't that about as good as it gets? When someone says, "You rock," they're saying that you deliver, you get results—you make things happen and you look good doing it!

When I tell someone that she's being a rock star, I mean that her performance is top-notch and that it's apparent that she loves what she does.

She makes her job look fun and effortless. *"You are such a rock star!"* The expression connotes the image of a confident, self-assured performer at the top of his game. A *rock star* is a person living his dream—doing what he is obviously meant to do. Living large and loving it!

Rock stars are in the enviable position of being able to tell stories through their music. They help make memories for people, and usually, they make you feel really good—whether you're grooving to a song on the radio or your iPod or you're seeing the rock star at a live show. Most rock stars achieve a kind of immortality that the average person can only dream about. Hey, I wanna be a rock star, too!

Rock stars are treated better than royalty. Everyone wants to be a part of their inner circles. (That's where groupies came from!) People wait in line for hours for a glimpse of them and then shell out hundreds of dollars to see them perform. We want to be around them and breathe their rarified air. Rock stars have a vibe—a magnetic, almost magical quality—that surrounds them.

Most rock stars have that charismatic power and influence. Groups like the Beatles had an enormous effect on culture, and Frank Sinatra was the ultimate rock star of his era. But being a rock star goes beyond the adulation and fame and popularity. It's more than that. It's more than loving what you do and being incredibly good at it. It's more than making your work look like play. Think about it: Rock stars can actually make a difference and change the world!

Take U2's Bono and his extensive charitable and humanitarian work. Bono uses his worldwide fame and influence to truly make a difference in the lives of millions. In the '80s, rock stars like Bob Geldof and John Cougar Mellencamp helped stage worldwide charity events such as Live Aid and Farm Aid. Today, groups such as U2 and REM still wield significant influence on world events and humanitarian issues.

The celebrity status and star power of rock stars is rivaled only by movie stars and sports figures. After all, isn't Tiger Woods the rock star of his sport? Isn't Tom Brady a rock star? Even political candidates have sometimes been hailed as rock stars. Look at Barack Obama in the 2008 presidential election. He won in a landslide. Being called a rock star is pretty much the highest honor you can bestow on a person.

So how do you become the equivalent of a rock star in *your* world? How do you bring rock star magic to your business? "You rock!" What do you need to do to hear those two little words? Let's look at what it takes to achieve rock star status in your chosen profession.

Think of some of the greatest rock stars out there. What do they have in common? Well, they all work hard. They practice. They put in the time and effort to master their craft. In fact, even most "overnight successes" have been working at it for years and years.

Obviously work ethic is huge. To become the best at something, you have to work harder than the next person. That means thousands of hours of practice until you are the best. In Beijing, I saw the men's doubles tennis finals. Roger Federer was determined to win for himself, for Stanislas Wawrinka, his tennis partner, and for his country. You could tell how much Federer wanted the gold medal, and you could see how the years of hard work and practice paid off. Federer had an extra gear that most other players only dream of, and that gear made the difference in the victory.

My team at TicketCity often works eighteen-hour days. They ride at dawn during the Final Four, the Masters, and the Super Bowl. This work ethic leads to great customer service and amazing moments. After the workday, they go out for a nice dinner to recharge and plan for the next day.

Rock stars have charisma, energy, passion, and commitment. The musicians who succeed and survive show up night after night. They do what they say they're going to do. The good ones don't let their fans—their customers—down. Not surprisingly, hard work, commitment, energy, and passion are the same qualities any of us need to succeed—in life and in business.

The greatest bands in the world also know a thing or two about teamwork. They've got to be in sync, or they will end up sounding like a train wreck! When the teamwork and chemistry dissolves, as it did with the Beatles, the music ends. You've either got to pull together or you'll be pulled apart. Sometimes you have to work together to reinvent yourself and your company, like Steve Jobs, Jonathan Ive, and a team of engineers did at Apple with the iPhone. The times they are a-changing! You have to get out in front of the curve and stay ahead of the game.

Great rock stars are also consistent. Whether you buy a CD or go to a concert, you usually know what you're going to get. Okay, maybe not always, but most of the time rock stars are going to play their hits and deliver the goods. There's an unwritten promise between the star and the audience; it's an unspoken (or unsung) vow. As a customer, I'll gladly fork over my cash to see rock stars perform live, but I expect them to deliver an unforgettable performance and a memory to last a lifetime. If you're a rock star and you don't keep that promise, I'll keep my cash and skip your show next time you're in town! Inconsistency or under-delivery breaks that sacred promise.

It's the same with any business, but in many cases the promise is *not* unspoken. In fact, it may be in writing—and it's certainly promoted! When you make your promise to your customer—whether it's "absolutely positively overnight" or "the ultimate driving machine"—you damn well better deliver! It doesn't matter if it's a hamburger or a Hummer. Each product or service comes with an intrinsic promise—an implied guarantee. A McDonald's hamburger should taste the same whether you're in Dallas, Texas, or Dublin, Ireland. Expectations—promises—must be met. If my FedEx doesn't arrive absolutely positively overnight, you can bet I'm going to switch to UPS or DHL. When your business makes a promise, you must also deliver. It seems simple enough, but talk is cheap. Results are what count.

For the rock star, that means show up, play the hits, wow the crowd, and leave them wanting more. Of course, there will always be those mercurial artists whose bad behavior is practically part of the act. Maybe you *don't* know what you're gonna get these days if you plunk down your money to see Axl Rose or Amy Winehouse. Perhaps that's half the fun! But for these rock stars, as in business, customers will put up with those antics for only so long.

Consistency is crucial. Once you've developed that brand promise, you can't let your customers down. It's all about stability and reliability. In my company, consistency shows up in the form of my daily huddle—the brief morning meeting I have with my managers every day. Those daily meetings, along with our weekly management meetings and quarterly off-site retreats, provide the consistency and communication needed to ensure that we're all going in the same direction.

Being consistent also means being systematic. Execution should be part of your strategy. You need processes and systems in place to make sure the trains continue to run on time. I was talking with a colleague of mine who just opened up a new Austin restaurant, Mighty Fine Burgers, Fries, and Shakes. He was telling me why their lemonade is so popular. It's their system, he revealed. Every time they make a batch of lemonade, it must be mixed 300 times. Not 298. Not 305. But 300 times, every time. That's a practice and a process that makes good lemonade—and good business.

Of course, the flip side of consistency is reinvention. And rock star stalwarts also use reinvention and rebirth to stay fresh and relevant. Think back to how many different looks and sounds Madonna has had over the years. She was never one to shy away from experimenting. She kept pushing the limits and reinventing her "brand."

Yes, even rock stars have their own brand identity. Most bands are brands! A brand means something. It evokes certain feelings and images and beliefs. Brands—like great bands—are memorable. Is your company memorable? Do you have a strong brand identity? What does your brand stand for?

The Lyle Lovett brand is nothing like the Guns N' Roses brand, which is nothing at all like the Celine Dion brand! In any case, these artists have carved out a niche and created a brand identity—something any successful business must do. Once you've developed your brand, then you've got to market and promote to create *demand.*

CHAOS WARFARE

"What the heck is chaos warfare?" you're probably wondering. Simple: It's that feeding frenzy you create when you've got something that everyone else wants. Rock stars have it in spades. They're able to create that frenzy, that sense of urgency, that demand. You've just *got* to get tickets to that Bruce Springsteen show! Your daughter *must* go to the Hannah Montana concert! You absolutely *have* to see your alma mater in the Final Four! To maintain your social status and keep your ego intact, these are "must attend" events.

That's what my business is all about. Supply and demand. On the supply side, it's when the clock is always ticking and you've got to work that frenzy to your advantage. Think of the excitement and the adrenaline of a live concert. That's the kind of electricity at the core of chaos warfare.

Think Apple and the iPhone. Apple created such a feeding frenzy for its new product that the lines to grab one of the first iPhones were a mile long. Anyone who was an Apple fan had to have one, and they would do just about anything to make sure that they were one of the first to own it.

Sometimes chaos warfare is an illusion. The demand may not be real, but the *perceived* demand is so great that the need is intense. In the early days of my ticket business, when I was selling tickets out of my car, if I had one or two people looking for tickets, things were relatively calm. But as soon as I had eight or nine people waiting in line clamoring for tickets, the chaos warfare began! The feeding frenzy intensified. As buyer excitement and anxiety increased, so did the price of the tickets! That's the kind of demand we like, and it's the kind of demand you must create for your products or services. Have you ever been to an auction? The auctioneer does an incredible job creating and intensifying chaos warfare. You can feel it!

Believe it or not, high school boys' state basketball in Texas always has a feeding frenzy around it. The final four teams in divisions 1A–5A win their regional playoff games one week prior to the state tournament. Fans of these teams usually have not purchased tickets in advance, and when their team makes it, the frenzy begins. Fans from twenty schools are now desperately hunting for tickets to the games, and only a few seats are available because many have been sold in advance. The phone lines always light up and the frenzy begins.

The same thing happens when tickets for the band Phish goes on sale. Phish is one of the most successful acts in the music business, but their success is not from album sales—it's from live shows. Phish has played thousands of concerts over twenty-one years, but they've never played the same set list twice, which is one of the reasons that they were one of the highest grossing bands in the world when they were at the peak of their popularity in the mid to late 1990s. The band encouraged fans to tape the concerts and trade the tapes, which built up the band's name and popularity. The band was so popular in 1996 that their concert at the Red Rocks Amphitheatre overwhelmed the nearby town, and the band was banned from playing that venue for ten years. Phish proves that there is always a market for great live performances.

The biggest frenzy I ever saw was the 2008 BCS championship when Louisiana State University (LSU) barely squeaked into the Sugar Bowl. But all the stars had aligned for LSU. They won the SEC championship, and the championship game was to be played in New Orleans, Louisiana, their home state, against one of the best traveling football teams, the Ohio State Buckeyes. Our website went nuts and so did our phone lines. Tickets were going for $1,300–$5,000 for the game.

Everyone wants a seat at the best restaurant in town because everyone thinks it's the best restaurant in town! If you've ever been to Joe's Stone Crab restaurant at South Beach in Miami, then you know what I'm talking about. Sometimes the wait is as long as five hours! The service is amazing, the waitstaff is professional (many waiters have worked there more than twenty years), and the food is extraordinary. Chaos warfare rules are in effect at Joe's Stone Crab, so you'd better tip your maître d' or you'll have to wait a long time!

It's the same concept at work when there's a long waiting list for an appointment with the best stylist or hairdresser in town—the stylist is "in demand." The ticket business survives and thrives on that demand. If a big sporting event or popular concert is sold out, that's where we come in. (And it's why we insist that it's not sold out until we say it's sold out!)

The feeding frenzy ensues, so people call us at 1-800-SOLD-OUT. Our business model is predicated on that psychology of demand. Maybe a customer calls us and finds out she's ninth or tenth in the queue. Obviously, she's going to realize that there's a pent up demand, and that those ten callers in front of her are all vying for the same tickets! The supply is limited, and the demand far outweighs the supply. On eBay, during the final seconds of an auction, the chaos warfare takes over. That's where you see the most action on the auction item.

In the ticket business, you've got to not only create demand, but then you also have to be sure you can handle the demand you've created. It's like being in the pit at the New York Stock Exchange. If you can't handle the heat, get out of the kitchen! You've got to manage that delicate balancing act of supply and demand. You've got to work that chaos warfare to your favor. Are you ready?

Let's say you have a product like a hotel room or, in my case, tickets. These products are perishable. If a hotel room—or a concert ticket—goes unused, that potential revenue is gone forever, along with any additional revenue that could have come with it!

"Spoilage" is the scourge of many an industry, mine included. I learned early in my career that too many unsold tickets will sink your business faster than you can say "sold out." I recall one particular instance when I had four $40 tickets that I was about to eat. Believe me, $160 was a lot of money back then, and I acutely remember the sense of urgency. I had to sell those tickets. If I didn't unload them, I'd be stuck with worthless tickets. So I actually went down to the venue and sold the tickets for whatever the market would bear.

That same urgency and pressure exists today, only the numbers are bigger! As I pull up my ticket inventory board today, I've got at least $100,000 worth of tickets for events taking place in the next few days. This week, for example, we have tickets for Leonard Cohen in Austin, Texas, tonight and Thursday; Jerry Seinfeld for two shows this Friday; the band Slightly Stoopid on Saturday night; and Bruce Springsteen on Sunday. We also have tickets for the NCAA Final Four games on Saturday and Monday, as well as the Masters beginning next week. All these tickets need to be sold, or the potential revenue is lost forever. So even today I try to instill that sense of urgency into the business. Like any rock star, being successful in business means you've got a new audition every day. You're only as good as your last performance.

In my business—in any business—you can't get complacent. You've got to keep your eye on the ball. Since TicketCity is dealing with tens of thousands of dollars worth of event tickets on a daily basis, it's easy to lose that edge, that urgency. It's my job to motivate our staff to get those tickets sold. The clock is ticking. I'm not going to rant and rave, but I am going to ask why the tickets weren't sold yesterday. I'm going to keep an eye on our inventory for tomorrow and for the next week. Fortunately, I've got a great team that works together to make sure most of this inventory gets sold. That's how we've stayed in business and grown over the last eighteen years!

Ticket prices for big rock shows can really escalate. U2 has played Madison Square Garden several times when tickets have been upwards of $2000. The Rolling Stones have played private benefit shows in which tickets sold for almost $20,000 a pair. It all comes down to supply and demand.

THAT'S THE
TICKET!

SUPPLY AND DEMAND: THE MOST EXPENSIVE CONCERTS/EVENTS EVER

How bad would you want tickets to these shows? Well, lots of people must have wanted them really badly because they drove the demand—and the price—into the stratosphere.

5. Barbra Streisand in Las Vegas, December 31,1993 and January 1, 1994— $1,500 each; $5,000 for tickets in the secondary market
4. Texas Longhorns vs. USC at the 2006 Rose Bowl—$1,500 each; up to $3,500 in the secondary market
3. New England Patriots vs. Philadelphia Eagles in Super Bowl 2005—$3,250 each
2. The Masters featuring Tiger Woods (his first)—$12,000 for one badge!
1. Olympic Opening Ceremonies in Beijing—$15,000 per ticket!

Rock stars love praise; they love the ego boost and the rush that comes from being idolized and admired. And when the rock stars on my team perform well, I make sure that I heap on the praise. I strongly believe in sharing the credit and taking the blame.

Be generous in your praise. Recognize and reward your star players. Give them a chance to be center stage, like the rock stars that they are. Shine the spotlight on them and give them their moment. Everyone loves to be honored, so don't be afraid to provide that ego boost when it's warranted. A little love goes a long way!

IMPROVISE!

Rock stars can teach entrepreneurs and business people a lot about improvisation. As you can imagine, these top performers have to "wing it" occasionally, and they need to keep playing without getting flustered. We've all heard the phrase, "the show must go on!"

Certainly, great musicians have to be able to make changes on the fly in the midst of a performance. Anything can happen at a rock concert, and the star on center stage needs to be totally unflappable. This was the case during a U2 show in the old Boston Garden when a huge lighting truss (over the audience) partially gave way. The lighting rig was dangling precariously above the crowd, but lead vocalist Bono took control of the situation immediately.

Without missing a beat, Bono went from rock star to rescue hero by stopping the show to help clear out the audience members who were seated under the dangling lighting truss. He handled the emergency with ease and prevented an all-out panic in the crowd. The lighting truss was repaired quickly, the crowd returned to their seats, and the show continued.

"Improv" is a key skill for both performers and business people. You need to be able to react and adjust quickly in the midst of any event. You've got to know when and how to change the rules when the old rules aren't working.

My team has been involved in events where we had to adjust on the fly and change our plans quickly. In the supply-and-demand world of the ticket business, we've got to turn on a dime and constantly adjust to stay

THAT'S THE TICKET!

SCORING CONCERT TICKETS

Getting rock concert tickets is tricky. The band always holds tickets back for VIPs and media, and they sometimes release tickets the day of the show, so if you are fearless and don't mind being patient, you can get great seats at the last minute. If you are a huge fan and don't want to risk missing the show, try a broker like TicketCity. Ticket brokers often own season tickets at these venues and thus have some of the best seats in the house. Fans can also try eBay, StubHub, or Craigslist.

in business. On one occasion at the Masters, the admission badges had ballooned to $12,000! We changed the rules and started buying anything we could, including worker badges and journalist badges! When your company's motto is *"It's not sold out until we say it's sold out,"* then you've got to get creative and find a way!

During one Final Four event in Tampa, the tickets that we sold for $1,200 each had blown up to $3,000–$4,000 each! Again, we changed the rules by buying single tickets from anyone and everyone, including the coaches! By piecing the singles together and getting creative, we were able to buy the tickets for $500 each, fill our orders, and still make money. Of course, you plan and prepare, but you should always be willing to scrap those plans if the situation calls for it! Be quick on your feet. Adjust. Adapt. Improvise. Simply find a way!

That's certainly what I did when I wanted to attend a lavish private party featuring a concert with Prince. The tickets to the exclusive event proved impossible to get. The party was the talk of the town, and everyone wanted to be invited. Unfortunately, I was not invited, and even the owner of the venue couldn't sneak me in! This was a million-dollar event with unbelievably tight security.

I know it's hard to believe that *the* ticket guy, the guy who just received a key to the city from the mayor, could not crack this shindig! Apparently, there are still some things that money can't buy. So I did what any desperate, self-respecting entrepreneur would do. I changed the rules. I got creative. I knew a guy with the catering company that was providing the food for the event, so I simply pretended to be one of the caterers and snuck in with them! Yup, I was forty-three years old, sneaking into a concert by posing as a waiter. That's winging it! The moral of the story is "Do what it takes to follow your dreams."

KEEP YOUR BALANCE

For a passionate guy like me who typically lives life at 100 miles per hour, sometimes it's hard to remember to slow down. But it took a rock star to remind me that it's not necessary to be going "fast-forward" every waking minute!

TEN WAYS TO BE A ROCK STAR

1. Show up! Keep your promises and commitments no matter what!
2. Think of every day as an audition for your greatest gig.
3. Band together and leverage your team members' individual skills and talents.
4. Don't forget to play your greatest hits. Take what you are known for and deliver on expectations.
5. Leave your ego at the door.
6. Give your other team members room for "solos." Let them shine.
7. Leave it all onstage. Give every day everything you've got!
8. Treat your clients like VIPs and give them "all access" passes to you and your business.
9. Say "thank you" (a lot!), and show deep appreciation for your fans.
10. Make the world your stage and give the performance of a lifetime!

Always remember: How you do *anything* is how you do *everything*!

I recall one great show when I was invited backstage to meet the artist: Chris Isaak of "Wicked Game" fame. I was pumped. It was a great show, and I was excited to meet Chris. I was going my usual mile a minute—practically bouncing off the walls. (No, there were no drugs or alcohol involved—I'm just high on life!)

When I had a chance to meet Chris, I was flying: "Hey, man, great show! Wow! Thatwastotallyamazing!Thatwascoolwhenyou—" Isaak interrupted me: "Randy, slow down, man! You're making me dizzy. Just chill!"

It took this rock star to make me understand that you don't always have to be up 100 percent of the time. You don't always need to run as fast as you can. Sometimes, you gotta slow down to speed up. Take a step back. Breathe. Think. Look at your options. Make measured decisions.

When you work out hard at the gym your muscles get the benefit of growing, even when you're resting the next day. Remember feeling the pain after a great workout, and never forget that downtime allows you space to think and grow.

It's another great business lesson, because we're usually taught to be decisive and make quick decisions: Think on your feet. Move fast. Don't delay. What I realized talking to Chris Isaak that night was that no matter what you're doing, you have to be in balance. Slow down long enough to assess the situation. You can still act fast, but don't act rashly! Speed for speed's sake doesn't always make sense. Slow down. Find the balance. Not everything is a sprint to the finish. Sometimes, it's a marathon. Pace yourself!

That's why I'll always remember that great Van Halen concert with my kids. It's possible to balance work and play. You can sometimes marry business time with family time. Set your boundaries, know your limits, and keep your balance. You can be both a rock star *and* a normal guy.

AMAZING PROFILES: JOHN CALIPARI

John Calipari, the 2009 *Sports Illustrated* Coach of the Year, has spent two decades inspiring players on both collegiate and NBA courts. Calipari has led his teams to over 400 victories, making him the second-most winningest coach in college basketball. He's achieved his success with drive, determination, and a willingness to take chances.

His teams have made eleven NCAA tournament appearances. They have reached the Sweet Sixteen seven times, the Elite Eight five times, and the Final Four twice. In 2008, Calipari led his Memphis Tigers to the NCAA championship game, his one and only appearance. He has coached five teams to the NIT, winning the NIT championship at Memphis in 2002. He is one of only four coaches in NCAA Division I history to direct two different schools to a number one seed in the NCAA Tournament.

Calipari began his head coaching career with the University of Massachusetts, where he led his team to a number of conference titles and NCAA Tournaments, as well as coaching the team to its first number one national ranking.

After eight seasons with UMass, Calipari joined the NBA's New Jersey Nets as head coach. He had less success at the pro level than in college coaching and was fired by the Nets after the team started the 1998 season with just three wins and seventeen losses.

Calipari returned to college coaching in 2000, where he began a long and illustrious career with the Memphis Tigers. Calipari is credited with revitalizing the basketball program in Memphis, where he won 253 games, posted nine consecutive 20-win seasons (including an NCAA record four consecutive 30-win seasons), and earned nine consecutive postseason bids. His 2007–2008 team's thirty-eight victories set a new NCAA Division I men's basketball record for most victories in a season. His nine consecutive 20-win seasons and nine consecutive postseason appearances are the most in Memphis school history. He was named Conference USA Coach of the Year in 2006, 2008, and 2009.

Calipari is known for the "Memphis Attack," a revolutionary "dribble-drive motion" style of play first utilized by Pepperdine coach Vance Walberg. But Calipari has perfected the style, racking up an impressive 252-69 record in nine seasons with Memphis.

Just a few days after the season-ending loss in the 2009 NCAA Tournament, Calipari agreed to become the head coach for the University of Kentucky, with an eight-year contract reportedly worth over $31 million! Coach Calipari's combination of charm, charisma, and chance taking will likely add up to success as he begins his career with the Kentucky Wildcats.

RULE #10
FOLLOW THROUGH.
MASTER THE GAME.

Only one who devotes himself to a cause with his whole strength and soul can be a true master. For this reason mastery demands all of a person.
—*Albert Einstein*

IN 1997, TIGER WOODS WAS PLAYING his first Masters as a professional, and the general public was full of Tigermania. Nike Golf was sponsoring Tiger Woods and wanted to provide many of their clients with Masters badges so they could showcase their new line of golf products. The great quantity of badges that Nike needed caused the secondary ticket market price for the badges to skyrocket. TicketCity was able to help Nike obtain many of their badges, which cost upwards of $10,000 each. Tiger won the Masters in a remarkable performance and showed the world a glimpse of his incredible ability that would later dominate the game of golf.

I saved this chapter for last because, if you've followed the advice and examples from the previous chapters, then you're on the path to mastery.

And mastering the game is what it's all about. As long as you're always learning, growing, and self-improving, you're on the way to mastering the game.

THE MASTERS

To become a master takes years of practice, hard work, dedication, and focus. The famous golf tournament known simply as the Masters is the premiere golf event in the world, and one of only four major championships in men's professional golf. The Masters is considered an official money event on the PGA Tour, and it is always played the first week of April at the Augusta National Golf Club in Georgia. As you can imagine, you've got to be a true master to compete at the Masters.

In 1934, when Clifford Roberts and Bobby Jones first established the Masters tournament, the winner received $1000. The 2009 champion, Argentina's Angel Cabrera, won in a playoff and took home a cool $1.35 million; the total purse in 2009 was $7.5 million.

The Masters is known for its distinctive green jacket donned by the winner. It's one of those famous traditions that makes the Masters unique, and it makes the tournament a coveted prize among the world's best golfers. The Masters has the smallest field of all the major championships, usually about ninety players. It is an invitational event, with invitations largely issued on an automatic basis to players who meet special criteria. The top fifty players in the Official World Golf Rankings are all invited. It is truly a one-of-a-kind event!

Tickets for the Masters are incredibly difficult to come by, and even the practice rounds can be tough to get into. Applications for practice round tickets have to be made nearly a year in advance, and the tickets are then distributed by lottery. Tickets to the actual tournament are sold only to members of a patrons list, which is closed. A waiting list for the patrons list was opened in 1972 and closed in 1978. The waiting list was reopened in 2000 and subsequently closed once again. In other words, unless you have friends in high places (like us!), it's unlikely you can get a ticket to this exclusive event. (But now you've got an inside track with TicketCity!)

As part of TicketCity's drive toward mastery in terms of customer service, we go above and beyond to make sure that our Masters attendees have

THAT'S THE TICKET!

ATTENDING THE MASTERS

The Masters championship takes place over seven days. The first three days, from Monday to Wednesday, are practice rounds. Fans can take pictures during these rounds. The par three tournament held on Wednesday is very popular with fans. On several of the par three holes, some players try to skip their golf balls over a water hazard and onto the green. Tickets for the practice rounds range from $250 for Monday's round to $350 for Wednesday's round. The regular rounds of the Masters begin on Thursday and go through Sunday. A badge is good for all four days, and it only costs $200—if you have had it in your family for the last forty years. If not, you have to buy a badge on the secondary market, and the average price is $4000, or about $1000 each day. In past years when the economy has been in good shape, it is not unusual for a daily badge to average $2000 each day.

A Masters golf badge is truly one of the most difficult tickets to obtain in all of sports. Golf fans love their sport, and with perhaps 35,000 fans allowed to attend each day, there is not a lot of availability. If you are not one of the lucky few who owns badges for the event, you can still apply for practice rounds, which are sold through a lottery process. And you can always order tickets and hospitality online through TicketCity.com

the most incredible experience ever. In fact, we even purchased a home on the famed Azalea Drive, just steps from the hallowed gates of Augusta National Golf Club.

Owning a home near the golf course allows us to provide hospitality and exceptional service to our clients who are attending the Masters. It's about convenience and customer service. Our clients can stop by, have a snack or refreshment on the way to the tournament and then come by again on their way to dinner. What's even more appealing is that our clients can also park at the TicketCity house.

What else can we learn about mastery from this historic and revered golf event? If you want the distinction of being a master of your profession, you need to possess the drive and ambition to be the very best. You need a relentless pursuit of perfection—and you've got to be committed to ongoing growth and self-improvement. Just as the world's finest athletes continue to practice and work to improve their game, you've got to keep learning if you want to be a champion.

Observe the masters in action and model their success. Develop the same habits the masters use—passion, commitment, perseverance, and a tireless work ethic. Play the game with fairness and integrity—and maintain a positive and winning attitude. Rarely will you see someone at the top of his game complaining or slacking off. Winners show up ready to play and expecting to win. It's not arrogance, it's confidence.

Mastery also requires integrity and following your heart. Usually, if you are passionate about something, you're very good at it. So follow your passions, follow your heart, and stick to your values. Not only is it the right thing to do, but it will help you succeed! Don't quit! Have the heart of a champion!

Being a master, whether it's in golf or in tennis or in life, means you're well-rounded. You've mastered all aspects of the game. You've got a lot of skills you can draw upon. You've got the complete package. You need to understand your strengths and minimize your weaknesses.

As an entrepreneur and the head of a company, I see myself as the conductor, overseeing the orchestra. It's my job to make sure everyone is playing their part, but it's also my responsibility to make sure that my entire entourage is in the Loop of Love! That means a big part of my job is making my employees and customers feel good about themselves and their transactions. I've got to make sure they feel good about the entire process so they come back again.

When I'm at the Masters, it's like being at a great tailgate party. I hang out with clients on the deck of our house near the golf course, socializing and spending time with everyone. I've got to orchestrate the big picture and make sure everyone is having an amazing experience.

That includes my own team. I need to keep them motivated and at the top of their game. In China, during the Olympics, that meant making sure my employees were not getting too stressed out or burnt out. It was a high-pressure, long-hours grind, so it was my job to keep them healthy and happy. That's why we closed up shop at the end of one long day and I took everyone out for a huge dinner. It gave us a chance to catch our breaths and have some fun before we had to dive back into the work frenzy. The "band leader" has to continually take the pulse of the organization and decide when it's time to give the band a break.

One other important aspect of mastery is to make sure you've got a coach. It doesn't matter what level you're on—you need the support and guidance of a coach, or several coaches! Whether you're just starting out, or you're Tiger Woods or Bode Miller, having a coach to guide you will put you on the right path to mastery. Even if it's just a mentor to bounce ideas off of, having a personal coach is crucial to success.

We talked about this earlier in chapter 7, but it bears repeating. Don't try to go it alone. Find yourself a coach or a mentor and keep an open mind for learning. Even a master can still be a student. Bode Miller has an entire team of coaches. It's important to have that kind of support system in place as you follow the path to mastery. You'll get there a whole lot quicker with a coach!

However, keep in mind that mastery is not a destination; it's a journey. It's what you do *along* that road. It's doing things the right way. It's winning those daily, weekly, and monthly battles—but it's winning with honor, integrity, and courage. It's how you play the game!

PUT IT ALL TOGETHER

If you expect to master the game—and be at the top of your game—then you've got to put it all together. You'll want to take all of the success attributes we've been talking about and practice combining your strengths to become a true master in your profession. With that in mind, the following are ten qualities that lead to mastery. I have no doubt that you'll recognize some of these traits, since we've touched upon these keys to mastery throughout the book. Still, let this list serve as a reminder that real mastery means doing a lot of things right, and doing the right things amazingly!

COMMITMENT

Mastery takes commitment—serious, long-term, stick-to-it commitment. The first step to achieving any goal is to *decide* you're going to do it; then promise to yourself and to others that you'll follow through.

When you keep commitments, people know that they can count on you—and that trust builds success. It's the same with TicketCity. We make a commitment to our customers, and we consistently deliver on our promises to them. That way, the relationship becomes stronger and they come back to us the next time they need tickets. Keep your commitments! Keep your customers! It's a pretty simple formula, really, but it's not nearly as easy as it appears! Commitment is the first stepping-stone on the path to mastery.

DEDICATION

Dedication and commitment are often used interchangeably, but I believe that dedication is more than just commitment. It's about learning. It's about loyalty. When you are dedicated, you are present. And when you're present, you are committed to the moment, whether it's with friends, family, colleagues or customers.

Dedication is about learning and devoting yourself to self-growth and self-improvement. You've got to keep constantly learning and growing if you want to become a master. You can't ever think you know it all. Even the best can get better. Dedication is the ongoing pursuit of perfection.

EXECUTION

You can practice and prepare for months—or years—but if you don't execute, you're toast! Practice is half the battle, but performance is the other half. Execution is all about completing the task or challenge as planned. At some point, after all the preparation, you've gotta dive in and get it done!

When my team was getting ready for the 2008 Olympic Games in Beijing, we planned for months. We had meetings, strategy sessions, contingency plans, and daily huddles. We prepared meticulously, trying to play out every possible scenario. Going halfway around the world to an unfamiliar country for an event that happens once in a lifetime is a pretty big deal for a company like ours. So you can imagine that the stakes were high.

Still, once my team was on-site in China, anything could (and did) happen! No matter how much we planned, we still had to execute. We had to perform. We had to deliver. Things happened that we never could have planned for, but we reacted and did what we had to do. When the rubber meets the road—when it's go time—that's where execution comes in. That's when it's time to think on your feet!

CHANGE THE GAME

Masters are unafraid of changing the game. Steve Jobs is a game changer. He threw out the rule book and innovated an entirely new industry when he and Apple created the iPod. Changing the game takes courage and vision. Changing the game takes balls of steel, baby!

TicketCity changed the game in 1996 when we became one of the first ticket companies to put up a website and take orders online. Today, that's standard operating procedure; but back then, it took some audacity to change the game and go online before anybody else. Don't be afraid to take risks. Zig when others zag! If you think the game can go better, change the game!

PATIENCE

They say "patience is a virtue, sought by many, gained by few." Patience is indeed a very difficult quality to master, especially since patience can often be confused with indecision. As with anything, it's a delicate balancing act. My take on it is that you've got to know when to be patient and when to take action.

Sometimes, you have to slow down to speed things up. I was in a frenzy trying to find a new CEO for my company for over a year. Finally, when I slowed down, found some patience and took a step back, I found my new CEO—right in front of me! I simply promoted one of my own team members to the top spot and my problem was solved!

Warren Buffett is the king of patience. He sees hundreds of deals, but Buffet is patient enough to say no to almost all of them. However, he recently said yes to a $5 billion deal with Goldman Sachs. Watch this pay off for Buffett.

PERSEVERANCE

You'll never achieve mastery if you give up too soon. You've got to develop a dogged determination to reach your goals. Perseverance and persistence are vital ingredients for success.

While at the Summer Olympic Games in Beijing, I marveled at the athletes and their ability to reach deep inside to find that extra spark to push them over the top. Their steely resolve and fortitude was awe-inspiring. How does an individual like Michael Phelps win eight gold medals? How can one man be so dominant in his sport? Years of training, obviously, but Phelps also had strength of body, strength of mind, and unrelenting perseverance.

CORE VALUES

This is a biggie for me. Without honor, integrity, and core values, you are never going to gain true mastery. You've gotta walk the talk! What do you stand for? How do you create meaning in your life? Decide what's important to you and then live by it. Not just once a year on New Year's Day, but every day. Test yourself. Push yourself. Be honest with yourself.

I have a tickler in my Outlook calendar that goes off every Friday at 5 o'clock, without fail. It's a weekly reminder to me that says "reflection of core values." So every Friday afternoon, I take at least fifteen minutes to reflect, review, and recommit. I look over my list of core values to see how well I accomplished them each week. My list includes things like: Have fun. Live life passionately. Enjoy and spend time with my kids. Be a great parent. Continue learning and growing. Make money. Be healthy. Make a difference in the lives of others. See the world. Laugh as much as possible. So, *what's on your list?*

BALANCE

As you can see, I've got an ambitious list of core values. That's why maintaining balance is so important to success. If I don't strive for balance and some sense of harmony in my life, something is going to get all out of whack. It's not an easy thing to do for any of us. Life's demands get in the way, and there always seems to be a fire to put out at home or at work.

But being aware is the first step to achieving balance. For me, my Friday check-in helps me stop long enough to do a gut check on life. That way, I can see if any one area—home, work, family, health, finances—is in need of more time or attention. Balance helps you keep everything aligned and in perspective.

FEARLESSNESS

Live without fear. That means being willing to take risks, and not shying away from those things that are difficult or even unpleasant. Face your challenges head-on. Get into the trenches and dig in when you need to. Swim with the sharks if that's what it takes. Opportunities await but only if you've got the courage and boldness to dive in. Don't be afraid. Dive into the fear. If you do so, your fear will disappear.

PASSION

We're back where we started, with passion—a must-have ingredient for success and mastery. Passion drives you and keeps you "on purpose." It's why TicketCity is successful, and it's why some of the most amazing entrepreneurs are successful.

Just look at the way Sir Richard Branson throws himself into his endeavors, or how Steve Jobs at Apple continues to turn the industry on its ear with products like the iPod and iPhone. Steve Jobs doesn't need the money; he keeps going because he's driven by his passion.

Whatever you do, you've got to do it with passion and enthusiasm. Not only will it keep you going when things get tough, but it sets the tone for your entire team. When you're passionate and zealous, your exuberance will spread to the people around you. And when your team shares your passion, you can move mountains together!

Finally, don't give up. Never quit. Believe in yourself and your ability to succeed. Love what you do, do it well, and keep on doing it! Exude passion. Enjoy the journey. To illustrate that sentiment, here's a brief poem I wrote when I was young, but all these years later I still refer to it when things get tough:

> *When you're feeling down and blue, with deep regrets and sorrow, too*
> *You cannot sleep because you're not feeling right*
> *You cannot cry, but you do not know why*
> *Your thinking is erratic, because you're tired of the stuff in your attic*
> *What's going on?*
> *Life is no sweet love affair*
> *Life is a game of troubled times and hardships*
> *Sparkling moments only occur every so often*
> *But those times are what I live for . . .*
> *Good night. Now I can sleep*
> *For I am special.*

AMAZING PROFILES: JESÚS CHÁVEZ

The story of Jesús "El Matador" Chávez is a story of redemption. Chávez was born in Mexico, raised in Chicago, convicted of armed robbery at age sixteen, sent to prison, and then deported back to Mexico at age twenty. The story could have ended there, as it has for many young men with troubled lives. But Chávez fought back, both figuratively and literally.

Back in Mexico, Chávez found an immigration lawyer and began his fight to get back into the United States. When he was able to return to America, he embarked on an amazing boxing career, marked by both triumph and tragedy. His struggles to attain U.S. residency and to become a champion in his sport were chronicled in a documentary titled *Split Decision*.

Chávez moved up the ranks, racking up an impressive record of forty-three wins and just four losses. Along the way, he became the 2003 WBC Super Featherweight Champion and later took the IBF Lightweight Champion crown in 2007.

However, his greatest victory was marred by tragedy. Chávez defeated Leavander Johnson in an epic bout that was finally called by the referee. But Johnson lapsed into a coma after the fight and died five days later. Chávez would not get in the ring again for another year and a half, despite encouragement from Johnson's family to keep boxing.

"There hasn't been a time when I don't think about him," Chávez says, referring to Johnson. "I'm doing what I love to do, and Leavander was doing what he loved to do. I keep him in mind coming into every single one of my fights since then."

Eventually, Chávez did return to the ring, but he lost his IBF title to Julio Diaz in 2007. But in 2008, Chávez knocked out Andres Ledesma, improving his record to 44-4. Asked about his past and his adversities, Chávez says, "What I've told people is how to overcome obstacles in life and put stuff behind you and keep trucking. Life goes on and you have to make the best of it. My past has made me mentally a lot stronger and physically a lot stronger, and it makes me a better fighter."

Chávez has fought his way to the American dream and continues to live that dream today. He now lives and trains in Austin, Texas.

EPILOGUE

I started this book with my 100 Things to Do in Life List, and now I can cross one more biggie off that list: write a book. Check. Done. Wow, that feels good! What's next? The journey continues!

So, what's on your Things to Do in Life List? If you don't have one yet, I challenge you to make a list of one hundred things you want to do, be, or have before you die. Can't think of one hundred things? Start with twenty. Start somewhere. Just start! Now is the time to chase your dreams, pursue your passions, and go after your goals with purpose. You've got an all-access pass to an amazing life, as long as you're willing to use it. We're saving a seat just for you. That's your ticket to success! Get your ticket to the limit!

APPENDIX A
ALL ABOUT MY BUSINESS

Over our twenty years in business, we have seen a lot of change in the world of ticket brokers; it has grown from a few regional companies to a thousand ticket brokers and billions of dollars in transactions. Ticket prices have increased, operations that once relied on phone and fax now have sophisticated websites, and regulations limiting ticket resale have been abolished. The ticket industry continues to evolve and will drastically change over the next three years. TicketCity will continue to be a reliable source for good tickets and great service as we adapt to changes within our industry.

THE OPEN-BOOK PHILOSOPHY

One of the reasons TicketCity enjoys such low turnover and employee loyalty is that everyone knows everything! We have what I call the "open-book" policy. In other words, our books are open; we readily share company information with the staff; and the operation is completely transparent.

In that spirit, we'd like to tell you all about our industry. In the process, we can clear up some typical misconceptions about this fascinating business!

WHAT IS A TICKET BROKER?

A ticket broker is a business that sells tickets at market price. Market price is determined by the demand for a ticket and the price associated with obtaining that ticket. Market price fluctuates but is often higher than the face value printed on the ticket. There are thousands of businesses that sell tickets, but only a few hundred are ticket brokers, and only a handful of those have experience in the ticket industry. TicketCity is one of the largest ticket companies in the world and offers a wide range of services.

Ticket brokers sell tickets to events and specialize in providing premium tickets to sold-out events. Ticket brokers are service businesses that save clients time and make buying tickets easier. TicketCity clients can buy tickets to events that are not available through other channels, such as the Masters and single events that normally require purchasing an entire season or paying expensive donations to obtain.

What is the difference between a ticket broker and a scalper? Not much, if you ask some people, but the reality is that ticket brokers provide a valuable service. A ticket broker is an established business with a physical office location. Brokers provide benefits on par with any business: phone orders, credit card payments, and a stated refund policy. A ticket scalper is someone who buys and sells tickets directly outside a venue. Buying tickets from scalpers is a risky proposition because they only accept cash and do not offer refunds.

HOW TO FIND A RELIABLE TICKET BROKER

There are thousands of ticket brokers on the Internet, so how do you know which ones are reliable and can provide the tickets that you need? Below are a few requirements you should look for when trying to decide which ticket broker to use.

1. Check for hidden fees; some brokers hide their service charge until you have already provided your personal information.
2. Know who you are buying from; make sure they have an About Us page and easily accessible contact information.
3. Make sure they have a stated return policy.
4. Find out whether they offer a money-back guarantee.
5. Make sure they offer safe, secure ordering on the Web. Look for "https" in the URL of the order form and the secure "lock" symbol somewhere on the browser.
6. Ensure they offer a reliable shipping method.
7. Look for membership in the Better Business Bureau (BBB).
8. Verify that they have a stated privacy policy.
9. Buy from a ticket broker who has been in business for five or more years in order to benefit from the experience they have in comparison with new brokers.

HOW DO TICKET BROKERS GET THEIR TICKETS?

Ticket brokers buy tickets through the same channels available to you. Brokers buy directly from the team or venue, from season-ticket holders, from other ticket brokers, and they buy during public on-sales. Many of the tickets that TicketCity sells are seats they own by purchasing season tickets from teams or schools. The advantage TicketCity clients receive is they can purchase tickets to an individual game and do not have to buy the entire season or pay for a personal seat license (PSL).

Most ticket brokers own season tickets for various teams or venues; the brokers pay the same prices, fees, donations, and PSLs that everyone else does to acquire season tickets. The big advantage that TicketCity has in buying tickets is our years of experience. We have been in business since 1990 and have a network of connections with access to the best seats available for events all over the world.

DIFFERENCE BETWEEN PRIMARY TICKET MARKET AND SECONDARY TICKET MARKET

The team or venue box office is the primary ticket market. They print and distribute the tickets at face value plus service fees. Ticket brokers are part of the secondary ticket market; they resell at market value tickets purchased through primary vendors. Ticketmaster has a monopoly on the primary ticket market, as they have contracts to distribute tickets for a large number of the venues, promoters, and teams. Competition to Ticketmaster comes mostly from an army of small ticket distributors, but there a few large distributors, such as Live Nation, Tickets.com, and Telecharge, that sell for concerts, Major League Baseball, and New York theatre, respectively.

When you buy tickets, make sure you always check with both the primary source and a reliable ticket broker like TicketCity. The box office is the original distributor of the tickets, so those tickets will be available at face value, but box-office inventory is usually limited after the initial on-sale and might be entirely sold out. Before buying tickets, compare the options available through the primary market with the tickets available through a ticket broker because the broker tickets will be better seat locations and their prices are sometimes comparable. TicketCity often has ticket deals that are at or below face value because we own hundreds of season tickets that we have to sell, and occasionally demand on a particular event drops. Many consumers assume there is no value to be found from a ticket broker, but TicketCity has thousands of values available on our Ticket Specials webpage. In 2008, we were selling Super Bowl game-day tickets for as low as $1,200 each, an unheard-of price for an event of that magnitude.

For championship events, few tickets are ever made available to the public, so a reliable ticket broker is always going to be your best option when buying those tickets.

WHAT IS FACE VALUE ON TICKETS?

Face value is the price that is printed on a ticket. This price is established by the venue, box office, team, or promoter who handles the event. Most events are tier-priced, so there is an array of face values based on the quality of the ticket; an upper-level seat will have a lesser face value than a floor seat.

Ticket brokers sell tickets at market value, which is a price that reflects the demand for those tickets and costs associated with obtaining them. Mandatory donations, PSL charges, or other membership fees are often required to purchase tickets, so those additional fees are included in the cost of tickets.

Supply and demand drive ticket prices, which fluctuate just like commodities on the stock market; a hot event will sell for more than face value while a weekday Royals/Marlins baseball game could sell for less. Consumers often assume that ticket prices will decrease as an event nears, but often a short supply causes prices to go even higher.

HOW TO AVOID TICKET SCAMS

As in every other facet of commerce, there are unsavory people out there who will try to scam you when you are buying tickets, particularly when you are buying for hot events in high demand. The scammer may be trying to sell fake tickets, or they may be offering to sell tickets that they do not own. Ticket scams occur at the majority of big events, and some of the scams are so sophisticated that they are difficult for even an expert to spot.

One of the biggest ticket scams of all time was perpetrated by a shell company called BeijingTicketing.com. These guys took the money and ran. They took tens of millions of orders for the Beijing Olympic Games, and they never delivered a single ticket. During this infamous Web scam, they took orders for two years and then left their customers high and dry. Don't be fooled by similar shams!

Below are some tips that may help you avoid getting scammed when you are buying tickets:

1. If the deal seems too good to be true, then it probably is—so walk away.
2. Never pay with cash or a money order to buy tickets.
3. Be extremely careful when buying tickets on the street from a scalper.
4. Do not buy tickets that require you to wire money to a foreign country.

5. Be extremely careful buying tickets on free classified sites or auction sites.

6. Avoid buying from a ticket broker who is not reliable.

Many people ignore these rules because they want to save a few bucks, but they wind up losing a lot more when they fall victim to a ticket scam. Buying tickets from some anonymous person on the Web or a scalper on the street does not provide you any recourse if your deal is not legitimate.

Follow these guidelines when you are buying tickets:

1. Buy tickets from a legitimate source, a reputable ticket broker (see above).

2. Check the event, date, and time to ensure it is correct.

3. Know the location of the seats you are buying.

4. Understand when the tickets will be delivered to you.

5. Pay with a credit card.

APPENDIX B
TICKET GLOSSARY

Ever wonder what an LMT or PSL is? Do you know the difference between "cream seats" and "buried seats"? The ticket business has a language all its own, but now you can get the inside scoop with our complete Ticket Glossary. Here is a detailed listing of common *terms, abbreviations,* and *ideas* in the ticket industry. We hope this resource proves a valuable aid in helping you make good choices in your ticket purchasing. A glossary cannot cover everything, so please don't hesitate to call one of our sales representatives at 1-800-SOLD-OUT if you have further questions.

4-pack. A group of four adjacent seats.

Aisle seats. Seats located on the end of a row, seats adjacent to the aisle. These are preferred by people who want easy access to their seats.

Badge. Another form of a ticket that gains you entry to an event. The Masters golf tournament calls their passes "badges," rather than tickets.

Bar C. The lines on a ticket that are scanned to gain access to an event.

BBB. Better Business Bureau. TicketCity has been a member in good standing for more than ten years.

Blink. A fake, or counterfeit, ticket. You will not be able to get into the venue with a blink. Consumers need to be especially wary of these when buying tickets on the street outside the venue.

Blinkers. Plural form of *blink*.

Box office (BO). The original distributor of tickets for an event.

Broker. A ticket broker. A person or entity that can legally resell tickets for an event. TicketCity is a ticket broker.

Buried seats. Seats that are furthest from the center.

Burners. Tickets you use to get in to an event when you don't plan to sit in those same seats. People often use burners when they have access to a suite but don't have a ticket to sit in the suite.

Busted order. An unfilled ticket order. Buying tickets from a disreputable ticket company can lead to a busted order. TicketCity has a 200% guarantee on confirmed orders.

Championship events. Major sporting events like the Super Bowl, Masters, Final Four, Kentucky Derby, Olympics, and World Cup. TicketCity specializes in championship event tickets.

Consignment. Consignment is when tickets are sold on behalf of a client. If sold, then TicketCity pays a predetermined amount back to the client who owned the tickets.

Cream seats. Really good seats.

Duplicate tickets. Counterfeit tickets. You will not be able to get into the venue a duplicate ticket. Consumers need to be especially wary of these when buying tickets on the street outside the venue.

Eventtixx. TicketCity's proprietary ticket management software. Aka: EventTixx Software or Real Time Ticketing

Face value. The actual price that is printed on a ticket.

Facility fee. An additional charge on your ticket that is added by the ticket box office.

Fan club. Artists typically have a fan club that you can join to get access to special ticket offers or ticket presales.

Floor seats. Seats located on the floor at an event.

Fruit seats. Really good seats.

Garbage. Worst seats in the house.

General admission show. A performance where there are no reserved seats. You will not have an assigned seat.

Get ins. The lowest-price tickets for an event. They typically offer the bare minimum view of the event.

Gold circle seats. Some venues or shows label their premium seats as Gold Circle. Not used for all venues or shows.

Handling fee. An additional charge on your ticket that is added by the box office.

Hard ticket. Physical ticket

Heating up. Prices are going up for an event.

Hospitality. Special entertainment available at an event, usually at an additional charge. Hospitality often includes special food and drink options for free, or at a discounted price. TicketCity offers hospitality for all Championship Events, and many other events.

In-hand. Tickets are ready to ship.

In-stock. Tickets are ready to ship.

Intermission. Period between the acts at a theatre production or show.

Junk seats. Worst seats in the house.

Last minute transaction (LMT). A ticket order that occurs at the last minute, and requires the buyer to pick up from a location at the venue.

Local pickup. A ticket order that must be picked up at the venue for the event.

Luxury box. Also known as a luxury suite or suite. Exclusive area at an event that offers a great view and typically is fully catered. Make sure you inquire whether the catering cost is included in your luxury suite.

Market value. The price a ticket is sold at above face value. Market value is determined by what consumers are willing to pay for tickets (supply and demand).

Masked location. Exact seat locations with similar sightlines, but in a different location.

Mezzanine. An upper level of the venue.

NATB. National Association of Ticket Brokers, an organization for ticket brokers. TicketCity is not a member.

No oddlot. A group of tickets that can be sold only in even increments $(2, 4, 6)$, not in odd numbers $(1, 3, 5)$.

No splits. A group of tickets that cannot be split up. They must be purchased as a group.

Nose bleeds. Upper-level seats. Usually some of the highest seats in the venue.

Obstructed view. View of the event could be slightly obstructed. A pole, camera, screen, the roof, or some other object obstructs part of the view.

On-sale. The public distribution of tickets from the box office. Ticketmaster typically schedules on-sales for hot events on Saturday mornings.

On-site pickup. A ticket order that must be picked up at the venue for the event.

Parking pass. Access to a reserved parking area close to the venue. TicketCity sells parking passes for most events.

Personal seat license (PSL). Certificate of ownership of certain seats in a venue. You have to buy this in addition to buying the seats from the box office, team, or venue.

Piggyback seats. Tickets that have the same seat number in two adjacent rows.

Presale. Ticket presales occur when the box office sells a set number of tickets to fan club members or VIPs prior to the public on-sale.

Price per ticket. The price paid on one ticket. All prices listed on the TicketCity website are the price per ticket.

Primary ticket market. The original distributor of tickets for an event.

Promoter. Public organizer of an event. The promoter works with the artist or team and box office.

Quantity. Number of tickets available.

Rainout insurance. Event insurance available in case of weather-induced cancellation.

Real time ticketing. TicketCity's proprietary ticket management software. Aka: EventTixx Software.

Reseller. Someone who resells tickets for events.

Reserved seating. A performance where there are assigned seats.

Row. The location of your seat within the section. Low rows are desirable at most events, except for racing events.

Scalp. Slang for reselling a ticket.

Scalper. Common term associated with someone who is selling tickets outside of a venue on the street.

Season ticket holder. A person who owns seats for every game or event for a particular team or venue; these seats are in the same location each year.

Season tickets. Tickets that are purchased year-after-year and located in the same location for every game or event.

Seat number. The location of your ticket within your row. Center locations or aisle seats are typically popular.

Seating chart. The map that illustrates your location within the venue. TicketCity offers venue seating charts to help you find your exact seat location.

Secondary ticket market. Ticket resellers.

Section. The physical location of your seat within the venue.

Selling air. Selling tickets you do not have. Also called SPEC or speculative inventory.

Service charge. An additional charge that is added to the subtotal price of the tickets.

Session. One particular time frame for an event. For example, the Final Four has two sessions: a Saturday session that includes two games, and Monday's session when the championship game is played. When buying tickets, make sure you check to see if they include one particular session or all sessions.

Single. A single ticket that is being sold by itself.

Sold out. When there are no more tickets available at the box office for an event. TicketCity is a great resource whenever you encounter a sold-out event.

SPEC. Speculative inventory. Selling tickets you do not have. Also called *selling air*.

SPO. Special purchase order. Tickets that will need to be purchased at a later time to fill a sale.

Spoilage. Tickets that do not sell or that go unused for an event. TicketCity offers many ticket specials to try to move tickets at a low price so they do not spoil.

Squatters. People sitting in seats that they did not purchase tickets for. A squatter moves from a worse seat location to a vacant seat in a better location.

SRO. Standing room only. An area of a venue that has no assigned seating. You must find space and stand for the entire event.

Stage setup. The arrangement of the stage within the venue. The stage setup often varies for different performers.

Strip. A group of tickets.

Suite. Also known as a *luxury suite* or *luxury box*. Exclusive area at an event that offers a great view and typically is fully catered. Make sure you inquire about whether the catering cost is included in your suite.

Ticket auction. Tickets that are sold to the highest bidder.

Ticket book. A group of tickets.

Ticket broker. Someone who can legally resell tickets for an event. TicketCity is a ticket broker.

Ticket hustler. Common term associated with someone who is selling tickets outside of a venue on the street.

Ticket industry. The entire scope of the primary and secondary ticket market.

Ticket marketplace. A location that allows ticket buyers and sellers to meet up to sell tickets.

Ticket scanner. The device used to scan the bar code on a ticket, giving the holder access to an event.

Ticket stub. The portion of the ticket that is returned to the holder after an attendant rips a ticket upon entrance into the venue.

Ticketfast (TF). A trademarked system from Ticketmaster that allows tickets to be e-mailed and printed at home. There is a barcode printed on the paper that can be scanned to permit entry into an event.

Tout. The British term for a scalper.

Venue. The building that hosts the event.

Walk. The area outside of a venue where scalpers are commonly found selling tickets.

Wall bangers. Seats located next to the wall, furthest from center.

Will call. The pickup location for your tickets. The venue will call is a common place to pick up tickets for an event. The venue will call will be clearly labeled and located near the ticket window.

Wristband. A band worn on the wrist that is used to identify people who have special seating locations or who can access a VIP area.

ABOUT THE AUTHOR

Randy Cohen is the CEO (Chief Energizing Officer) of TicketCity, the ticket brokerage company he founded in 1990. Randy's company has consistently ranked as one of the top ten companies to work for in Texas. TicketCity has been recognized in the *Austin Business Journal*'s Fast 50, a list of the fastest-growing private companies, and as one of the top five businesses in the Entrex PCI (Private Company Index).

Randy got his start in the ticket business in 1988 as a student at the University of Texas at Austin. Randy began selling tickets to local events and quickly developed a reputation as the "go-to guy" for great tickets. With his client base growing rapidly, Randy launched TicketCity in 1990.

Eighteen years and more than 2 million tickets later, Randy is one of the best-known and most successful entrepreneurs in the secondary ticket market. Today, he continues to work to expand TicketCity's market share by focusing on acquisitions and by putting together large ticket deals.

Randy graduated from the McCombs School of Business at the University of Texas as well as the Birthing of Giants program at MIT. He is a member of the Entrepreneurs' Organization and active within the Austin community. He is the proud father of a young girl and twin boys.

ACKNOWLEDGMENTS

I would like to thank Lou Bortone for all of his hard work and research done on *Ticket to the Limit*. I would also like to thank my family, friends, and Ticket City peers for their support during this journey!